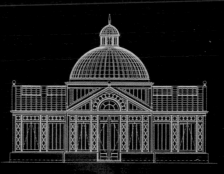

# INDIA JANE

page 248

page 214

page 128

# Contents

COUNTRY LIVING MAGAZINE

# Handmade STYLE

**EDITOR SUSY SMITH**
**Deputy Editor** Louise Elliott
**Art Editor** Lesley Straw
**Chief Sub-Editor** Michele Jameson
**Picture Editor** Jackie Swanson
**Advertisement Manager** Sara Leeson
**Sales Executive** Anastasia Mouskoundi
**Publisher** David Parker
**Group Publishing Director** Judith Secombe

HEARST magazines | UK
National Magazine Company

**HEARST MAGAZINES UK**
**Editorial Development Director** Ian Birch
**Director of Consumer Sales & Marketing** Sharon Douglas
**Chief Operating Officer** Anna Jones

**HEARST MAGAZINES INTERNATIONAL**
**President/CEO** Duncan Edwards
**Senior Vice President/CEO and General Manager** Simon Horne
**Senior Vice President/Editorial Director** Kim St Clair Bodden

**CHIEF EXECUTIVE ARNAUD DE PUYFONTAINE**

*Cover photograph by Simon Bevan*


Printed and bound by Polestar Chantry

*Susy Smith, editor, Country Living Magazine*

*Handmade furniture and furnishings have unique, individual appeal,* and perhaps never more so than in a world where cleanly machined, bulk-produced items have become the norm. Being able to see the chisel marks on a wooden bowl or the uneven edge where the dye has broken the fabric pattern is all to the good: this shows an item has been produced by hand and made with great care, usually by the designer. More importantly, it is a one-off. This ethos provided the starting point for this special *Country Living* bookazine in which we celebrate the beauty of bringing a sense of craftsmanship and artisan appeal to your home. Using material from the CL archives, we have created a world of ideas for lovers of both traditional and contemporary style. Inside you'll find beautiful decorating schemes, homes to inspire, projects to create and an array of makers from whom you can source beautiful, individual pieces.

If you like what you discover here, then why not join us at *Country Living* every month? There's a special subscription discount offer on page 290, so you'll never miss another copy.

*Susy Smith*

# Decorating
# IDEAS

*Adding elements of handmade style into your home is a surefire way to enjoy an individual interior. We show how to create a touch of utility chic, introduce fresh appeal with colour and pattern, and layer textures to feel-good effect*

RICHMOND · TUNBRIDGE WELLS · DORKING

STYLISH HOME ACCESSORIES

# MAISON

BEAUTIFUL HAND-PAINTED AND OAK FURNITURE

# MAISONHOMEINTERIORS.COM

# Utility chic

*Team natural woods with rustic textiles*

*and stone-coloured shades for a*

*beautiful, pared-down effect*

# Brown paper & string

Discover how these stalwarts of
the pantry and postroom can
provide the inspiration for subtle,
stylish decorating schemes

PRODUCED BY **HESTER PAGE**

PHOTOGRAPHS BY **JAMES MERRELL**

This palette can include delicate variations in colour, from mouse browns and greys to the lighter shades of wheat

## PERFECT PARTNERS

*The nostalgic quality of brown paper
parcels tied up with string was the starting
point for the beautiful decorating ideas
shown here. The subtle shades and textures
of classic packaging materials can be
found in a range of fabrics, papers and
colours for the home: in textiles such
as hessian and linen, in wallpapers
with textured finishes and paints with
names such as parchment or string.*

These natural colours will tone beautifully with handcrafted elements: simple wooden furniture, rustic baskets and rough-weave fabrics

Continue the look with practical accessories in interesting textures and natural materials such as handmade footstools

For a finishing touch, complement woven
pieces with galvanised metal accessories
— the ultimate in utility chic

# The country kitchen

The handcrafted, handmade look is providing inspiration for a growing band of designers. Discover how to add to the sense of simplicity with a palette of cool colours and individual pieces

PRODUCED BY **BEN KENDRICK**
PHOTOGRAPHS BY **BRENT DARBY**
AND **CATHERINE GRATWICKE**

# A clever conversion

Emma Milne-Watson has used ingenuity and vision to turn an old shed next to her Georgian rectory into a beautiful kitchen diner. A custom-made central work area, illuminated by industrial-style pendants, is covered with a pale, delicately veined marble. This has also been used for the worktops on the surrounding units and splashback, which is finished with a narrow strip of marble that serves as a shelf. With its expanse of white walls and abundance of natural light, the room has a feeling of pared-down beauty, while stripped beams, reclaimed parquet flooring (treated with white oil for a blond look) and an antique wooden dining table add warmth to the scheme.

A functional pantry area has been created in an adjacent room, with a walk-in larder, narrow antique wooden work table and a simple colour scheme characteristic of Scandinavian houses. The original terracotta pamment floor tiles have been restored and new glazed floor-to-ceiling cupboards installed to store provisions and Emma's collection of antique linens, china and glass. ▷

**SOURCEBOOK**
China, glassware and cutlery, **Ikea** (0845 355 1141; ikea.com). Posters by Patrick Thomas at **Outline Editions** (020 8451 3400; outline-editions.co.uk). Pendant lights, from a selection, **Idyll Home** (01630 695779; idyllhome.co.uk)

## design ideas

• A walk-in larder is a great choice if you have the space or can convert an area or even a large cupboard. Tiling the walls is a practical option and will help keep the room cool.

• Glazed cupboards appear much less obtrusive than normal panelled doors, but you do have to keep the contents harmonious and tidy. Or introduce colour and pattern by hanging fabric curtains to hide any clutter.

• Reclaimed fixtures and fittings are a good way to bring character to a newly decorated kitchen, but make sure they are compatible (particularly plumbing and electrics) before you buy.

# Let there be light

Several tiny rooms with sloping floors and low ceilings were knocked through to make one larger room in this 16th-century Sussex farmhouse. Renovation of the Grade II-listed property – including removing two to three tonnes of sandstone in order to lower the floor level – took four months and had to be carried out using authentic materials and building techniques. The original front door opened into the main space, so a porch was added with wattle-and-daub walls. All the beams had to be cleaned using a special poultice, as planning regulations would not permit sandblasting.

Owner Tony Fountain was keen for the room to be practical and hardwearing, as muddy boots come straight in from the farm outside. Appliances are hidden behind cupboard doors and a walk-in larder holds all the groceries, while a small island unit has a hob and cooker built into it so the Aga can be turned off in the summer. The finished kitchen has painted and natural wooden units alongside freestanding pieces, such as the dresser, which give the room an individual look.

# design ideas

• It is possible to combine natural and painted woods but this is best achieved if you keep a continuity of style throughout, and limit yourself to just one type of wood.

• In a larger kitchen, an island unit makes great design sense, creating an economical working area. The key is to make it appear as unobtrusive as possible and not allow it to dominate the rest of the space.

• If you're replacing a floor in an old property, either use reclaimed materials or try laying stone slabs (in this case, slate) in a random pattern to add character. ▷

## SOURCEBOOK

The English Classic range kitchen, **Mark Wilkinson** (01380 850007; mwf. com). Cumbrian slate floor tiles, **Honister Slate Mine** (01768 777230; honister.com). Polished marble worktops, **Burslem** (01892 750120; burslem.co.uk)

# Spacious & stylish

John and Emma Sims Hilditch's home in the
Cotswolds had once been the village school. Today,
the front has been transformed into an office for
Emma's interior design business, and, at the back, an
old tumbledown barn was converted into a spacious
open-plan kitchen-dining and living room, with
bedrooms and bathrooms above on a mezzanine level.

The barn needed complete restoration, including
levelling out the site and digging a trench to prevent
moisture from entering the walls. Now, this stylish
space is filled with brushed wood, marble worktops
and paintwork in calming shades of soft grey and
cream. All these natural elements combine to give
the area texture and tactile appeal, making it a
desirable place to work and relax.

Although the kitchen is essentially classic in
style, the cabinets have the latest fittings, such
as soft-close doors and drawers. It is the perfect
showcase for John's company Neptune, which
produces hand-painted wooden kitchens inspired
by Provençal and Scandinavian designs using
traditional joinery methods.

## design ideas

- A kitchen that is decorated with natural, neutral tones needs to incorporate a variety of surfaces, shapes and textures to keep it interesting.
- Marble worktops are beautiful and elegant, and will provide a cool surface, but spills, such as lemon juice, need to be dealt with promptly to prevent any stains.
- Drawers are much easier to use and access than normal cupboards, so when choosing your kitchen, consider fitting out units with runners and baskets or building solid-wood compartments ▷

**SOURCEBOOK**

Kitchen, furniture and accessories, **Neptune** (01793 427300; neptune.com). Interior design, **Emma Sims Hilditch** (01249 783087; simshilditch.com) Lighting, **Original BTC** (01993 882251; originalbtc.com). China, **Sophie Conran for Portmeirion** (01782 744721; portmeirion.co.uk)

# Relaxed & rustic

In this converted barn in Gloucestershire, Alistair Johnston and Tiny Nijman have created a classic country kitchen, where the sense of space and light shines through. The couple worked closely with their builder and kitchen company to produce a practical yet comfortable living area, with pale units complemented by the natural tones of solid wooden furniture and honey-coloured flagstone floors.

A few industrial-style elements look perfectly at home in this functional setting: an old factory lamp hangs over the central work unit, while scaffold poles act as curtain rods and also carry electric cables for porcelain pendant lights. Curtains in cotton ticking have a utilitarian simplicity that suits the kitchen and their metal eyelet headings add a stylish touch.

The kitchen incorporates lots of clever storage ideas including spice drawers, reminiscent of old chemist's shop fittings, and combinations of open shelving, glazed- and solid-door cupboards. A few well-chosen decorative pieces, papier mâché sculptures and Tiny's artworks make the room feel more homely. ▷

## SOURCEBOOK

Fitted, solid-wood painted kitchen, **Cotteswood** (01608 641858; cotteswood.co.uk). Prints and etchings, **Tiny Nijman** (07808 721754; tinynijmanart.com). Range cooker, **Britannia** (01253 471001; britannialiving.co. uk). Pendant light, **Hector Finch** (hectorfinch.com)

## design ideas

• If you are furnishing an open-plan kitchen that also serves as a general living area, try to keep any accessories simple rather than fussy.

• Never underestimate the amount and variety of storage you will need, from large cupboards for appliances, an ironing board or a vacuum cleaner to shelves or drawers to hold herbs, spices and small sundries.

• Always allow space to display a few decorative elements – these will soften the look of clean-lined cabinets and shelves, and add interest, too.

# Cool & calm

Extending the back of her Edwardian house in Surrey to accommodate a new dining area enabled Tamsin Crook to change the small, cramped kitchen she'd inherited for a much larger, open-plan one. Although it has a contemporary feel, the cabinets are classic in style and based on simple Shaker designs.

A long run of cupboards hides most of the appliances and much of the kitchen clutter, and some of the doors have been fitted with pull-out wire trays and drawers to make the contents more accessible. Keeping everything neat and tidy, or hidden behind the stone-coloured cupboards (painted in Farrow & Ball's Slipper Satin, Stony Ground and Skimming Stone to give a subtle but light feel to this north-facing room), gives the kitchen a calm, clean appearance, and helps it to blend harmoniously with the living area.

The large central worktop doubles as a breakfast bar and divides the kitchen from the living room on the other side, making this a much more communal space and enabling Tamsin to keep an eye on her three small boys while cooking.

**SOURCEBOOK**

Kitchen, **Adaptations** (020 8942 9868; adaptations.uk.com). Paints, **Farrow & Ball** (01202 876141; farrow-ball. com). High stools, **Heal's** (0870 024 0780; heals. co.uk). Blanco Norte compound worktop, **Silestone** (01256 761229; silestone.co.uk)

## design ideas

• An attractive rounded cupboard with a curved wooden worktop provides the kitchen with a much softer, more streamlined look than a traditional square-edged unit.
• Composite worksurfaces are robust and hardwearing, and are now virtually indistinguishable from natural stone.
• Position your sink or main worktop area where it will receive good natural light, preferably in front of a window where you can enjoy a view while you work.

The stone-coloured cupboards help
the kitchen to blend harmoniously
with the living area

# Home is where the *craft* is

An original handmade or traditionally crafted piece will give a room distinctive style, but it can also provide the starting point for a whole decorating scheme. We show you how to bring the maker's touch to your home and celebrate the beauty of British craft

STYLING BY **BEN KENDRICK**
ASSISTED BY **CELIA STUART-MENTETH**
WORDS BY **LOUISE ELLIOTT**
PHOTOGRAPHS BY **RACHEL WHITING**

## THE SCHEME

*In this kitchen, the warm, natural tones of Ray's hand-turned bowls are highlighted by being placed on crisp white linen and mirrored with an assortment of wooden pieces in similar hues to create a strong visual focus. The decoration has been kept spare and simple to emphasise the beautiful grain. These wonderful bowls would also work on a side table in a living area.*

Hand-turned wooden bowls, from £15 each, Ray Key at David Mellor (020 7730 4259; davidmellordesign.com)

# A natural palette

Wood-turner Ray Key's highly covetable, hand-crafted bowls are both beautiful to look at and a joy to use – the reasons why his range of domestic tableware has been stocked by cookware specialists David Mellor since the shop's early days. Based in Evesham on the border of the Cotswolds, he turns and smooths native woods, such as ash, elm and sycamore, with supreme skill to achieve a purity of form that allows the individual character of the timber, and its distinctive texture, to shine through. Ray also creates chopping boards, boxes, platters, dishes and vessels, as well as more sculptural designs, all inspired by his lifelong love of wood. Rustic simplicity at its best.

The geometric patterns of this hand-woven throw are an update of classic Shaker designs, and provided the starting point for this American Country-style bedroom. Crisp white linens and pale furniture offset the striking design, and the colours in the weave are echoed in other accessories, drawing it into the room.

Wool throw, £165, Melin Tregwynt
(01348 891644; melintregwynt.co.uk)

# Simplicity and style

This lambswool throw is made by the Melin Tregwynt mill in Pembrokeshire using a doublecloth weaving technique. Owner Eifion Griffiths is the third generation to run the mill, and every item made there needs specialist skills. Motifs range from classic designs, such as this St David's Cross, to more contemporary patterns in red and aqua spots and stripes.

# Tradition with a twist

A contemporary take on a classic country stick-back design, this chair is made for Baileys Home Store in Herefordshire using a range of traditional joinery techniques and sustainably sourced English hardwoods, including aged ash and elm. The seat is hand-carved into a shallow dish or saddle shape for comfort, the curved arms are steam bent and the legs lathe turned. The result is a form that pleases the eye and a structure that is strong and durable, while the wood is lightly oiled and will gain a beautiful patina with time. A chair to use and cherish.

Stick-back armchair, £620, Baileys (01989 561931; baileyshome.com)

## THE SCHEME

*One way to decorate with an eye-catching shape, such as this hardwood chair, is to complement its curved outline with strong silhouettes, such as the 1950s-style table, striking fabrics and contemporary lamp used here. The more traditional pieces soften the mood, with the warmth of the textiles bringing out the natural tones of the wood. Remember that it's easier to mix furniture from different sources if you keep the colour of the woods consistent.*

# JULIAN CHICHESTER

Regency Sofa in silver finish

# Colour
# & pattern

*Give every room fresh appeal with hand-*

*dyed fabrics, striking ceramics and*

*original hand-painted designs*

# IN DIGO
## *inspiration*

Natural dyes add an artisan feel and an incredible depth of colour to a room – and *indigo* is one of the most beautiful. The *blue* colour is extracted from various plants including woad, and has *beguiled* people through the ages with its deep, *inky* hue. This versatile shade has remained a source of *inspiration* for both fashion and *interiors*, whether featuring in hand-blocked linens, *batik-style* florals, rich ikats, utility tickings or casual *denim*.

STYLING AND WORDS BY **LAURA VINE**
ASSISTED BY **CAROLINE REEVES**
PHOTOGRAPHS BY **LISA COHEN**

Bring interest to a room by covering one wall or alcove with a striking floral wallpaper in a deep indigo shade. Partner with complementary checks and spots

## Blue is the colour

The natural qualities of indigo make it the perfect partner for weathered wooden floorboards and handcrafted pieces. For maximum effect, layer together fabrics, ceramics and accessories.

## Bold & beautiful
*Indigo is dark and inviting when used on its own or cool and crisp when set against a white backdrop – and always makes a striking statement.*

Echo the natural beauty of indigo with chairs covered in vintage linens,
patterned rugs and hand-printed materials used as simple cloths

## Mix & match

*A hand-stamped wall (opposite) introduces a unique patterned element. Here, a paisley motif applied in a deep indigo colour looks decorative without being overpowering. Dark blue walls may seem a bold choice (this picture) but, teamed with pale furnishings, they can create a sophisticated, inviting atmosphere.*

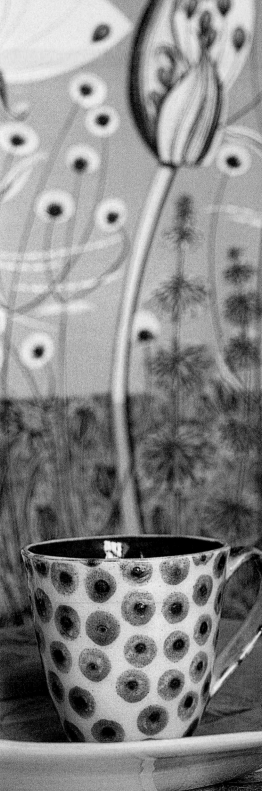

# DESIGNS
## *of the times*

Create a retro revival in your home with striking handmade ceramics, geometric textiles and graphic prints that capture the mood of the 1950s and 60s. Mix with simple Scandinavian-influenced furniture and plain bold fabrics in natural hues of teal, mustard and olive green

INTERIORS STYLING BY **BEN KENDRICK**
ASSISTED BY **CAROLINE REEVES**
PHOTOGRAPHS BY **EMMA LEE**

## ECHO THE STYLE
*Contemporary and vintage British artwork, such as bold, graphic woodcuts, linocuts and screenprints, suit this look. For pieces by famous illustrators and printmakers of the early 20th century, including Eric Ravilious and Edward Bawden, try Ben Pentreath (benpentreath.com) and Emma Mason (emmamason.co.uk). Also look out for Scandinavian furniture from the 1950s and 60s, particularly pieces by Hans Wegner, Eero Saarinen and Arne Jacobsen*

Team a geometric-patterned rug
and motifs drawn from nature
with upholstery and curtains in
solid statement colours

DEAL & WALMER

Offset the strong
sense of pattern and
design with plain
white woodwork and
simple rustic woven
chairs and baskets

Look for textiles and ceramics with repeating geometric patterns and stylised prints

## MADE BY HAND

*Many of the striking ceramics shown here, including the jug and small plate above, are by designer Katrin Moye from Nottingham (katrinmoye. com). Every piece is hand-thrown and hand-decorated with repeating motifs inspired by the patterns she observes in the natural world. From leafy greens to bold blues, colour is extremely important in her work, and her collection includes plates, mugs, jugs and platters, as well as large-scale collector's pieces.*

## FOLLOW A PATTERN

*Inspired by her interest in traditional British fabrics and textile crafts, Eleanor Pritchard (eleanorpritchard.com) creates a range of woollen blankets. The designs are tested on her dobby loom, then woven in a small Welsh mill. Eleanor uses a range of techniques to create her beautiful, distinctive patterns in soft, muted colours that suit the mid-century modern mood.*

A traditionally woven
blanket or floorcovering
will create an eye-catching
feature in a bedroom

# A *rosy* outlook

*With their velvety hues and array of shapes, roses are always one of the joys of summer. Enjoy their fleeting beauty for longer by filling your home with fabrics and accessories that capture this favourite flower's distinctive charm*

STYLING BY **CAROLINE REEVES**
ASSISTED BY **BEN KENDRICK**
AND **CELIA STUART-MENTETH**
PHOTOGRAPHS BY **EMMA LEE**

## Bringing the outside in

*Seek out furnishings and ceramics that celebrate the beauty of the rose, or try transforming plain tiles with your own hand-painted designs.*

From tiny sprigs to
full-blown flowers, a
rose design will convey
an instant sense of the
countryside

## *Faded charm*

*Use soft green paints and accessories to bring out the wonderful pinks of vintage roses, or create a contrast by offsetting the flowing, irregular patterns of floral fabrics and papers with neat stripes.*

## In the name of the rose

*Echo the colours and patterns of a hand-stitched quilt in an array of colourful cushions and throws. Cover an old box with a favourite rosy wallpaper for a pretty storage idea.*

# The decorator's palette

*Unite your scheme by looking for accessories and china with roses in similar hues. Give a simple chest of drawers a new lease of life with wallpaper sealed with varnish (opposite).*

# A brush with Bloomsbury

Adapt the exuberant decorating ideas at Charleston farmhouse to introduce touches of bohemian colour and pattern to your home

STYLING BY **CAROLINE REEVES** | ASSISTED BY **BEN KENDRICK**

PHOTOGRAPHS BY **EMMA LEE**

*For more than 50 years from 1916
onwards, Charleston, a farmhouse
on the South Downs in East Sussex,
was the country meeting place of
the Bloomsbury Group – a close-
knit circle of painters, writers and
intellectuals. Artists Vanessa Bell
and Duncan Grant set about
enlivening the dark, old interior
of the property by painting and
adorning every surface with
enchanting, naive graphics and
striking, country-influenced
images. Inspired by this unique
decorative style, we have created
our own interpretations of their
distinctive designs for you to follow.*

# Living room

*Be adventurous with colour and pattern – choose hues and shades from within the same tonal range to tie clashing designs together. Walls painted in neutral shades will allow these colours to stand out but not be overpowering. Add an extra dimension by painting onto a piece of furniture or a fire surround. The design here was done freehand using tester pots of paint, but a similar effect could be achieved with stencils or by tracing shapes such as lids and bottle tops.*

*Don't worry too much about making a mistake when decorating walls with a freehand design, as you can always paint over it*

# Hallway

*Balance a bold pattern in a small hallway by painting the area below the dado rail with a soft wash in a toning shade. Here, we sponged the paisley motif onto the walls with a stencil, and added a flower detail for extra effect.*

HISTOIRE NATURELLE

## Workroom

*An attic study is the perfect place to experiment with colour in your home. The strong shade of blue used for the exposed brickwork on this wall (opposite) has been toned down by the slightly paler shade chosen for the recess area. Lighter-hued furniture and accessories, with bright accents of mustard yellow and rust red, help to create a welcoming and relaxed workspace. Lay a woven floor runner with a distinctive pattern to pick up on the stepped outline of the brickwork.*

*Bloomsbury Interiors offers a beautiful range of hand-painted lamps, fabrics and furniture (bloomsburyinteriors. wordpress.com)*

## Kitchen

*Add interest to a white kitchen with a graphic, statement wallpaper above a plain, tiled area. Carry the colours through the room with accessories and china in a mix of vivid shades.*

# Bedroom

Emphasise the colours of furnishings and accessories in a bedroom by echoing their shades in a bold band painted around the top and side edges of a plain wall. Delicate freehand painting on the bedframe in toning colours will continue the theme and add an individual touch to a room. If you don't feel up to painting a design completely freehand onto the bed, use a stencil for the central motif and then add a few flourishes yourself for an original finish.

*This is a decorating look that can evolve gradually around the home as you develop more confidence in the power of pattern to change the mood of a room*

# Best of British

From potters and artists to woodturners and textile designers, Britain's talented craftspeople offer an array of unique pieces. Follow our inspiring ideas for creating decorative detail and interest using only home-produced products

FLORENTINES

BENTLEY & SPENS

STYLING BY **CAROLINE REEVES**
ASSISTED BY **BEN KENDRICK**
PHOTOGRAPHS BY **SIMON BEVAN**

**CONTEMPORARY CLASSICS**
*Wooden furniture that shows the signs of traditional craftsmanship, such as Ercol's steam-bent designs, brings a sense of heritage and style.*

## MATERIAL PLEASURES

Seek out handmade cushion covers and blankets in beautiful, eye-catching patterns – almost works of art in themselves. Echo their hues in an assortment of paintings.

THE TALE OF
SAMUEL WHISKERS
OR
THE ROLY-POLY PUDDING

BY BEATRIX POTTER
F. WARNE & CO.LD

**THE POWER OF PRINT**
Handprinted wallpapers or fabrics
will lend an artistic, original
quality to a room and a strong
depth of colour. For best effect, mix
designs around one basic shade.

**CHARMING CERAMICS**
Build up a collection of hand-
thrown china from a range of
country potters – rustic pieces that
are robust enough to use every day
but that will also please the eye.

As a nation, we have a long history of weaving wools and cottons - from simple stripes and spots to more elaborate decorative designs

# SOFA WORKSHOP

individual sofas, for individuals

# A touch of texture

*Use beautiful woollen accessories and*

*hand-woven baskets to create detail and*

*layers of interest in a scheme*

# The *warmth* of WOOL

*With its natural qualities and rustic charm, wool is the perfect partner for country interiors. We show you how to make the most of the wonderful ranges being produced by small cottage industries today – tweeds, plaids, throws, yarns and much more*

STYLING BY **BEN KENDRICK** | ASSISTED BY **CAROLINE REEVES** | PHOTOGRAPHS BY **EMMA LEE**

# Sitting room

Strong and hardwearing, British wool is the ideal material for carpets and keeps its colour well – Brockway offers a good range (brockway.co.uk). Top with a bold woollen rug for extra impact. Woven Shetland plaids in smart, sophisticated shades are a comfortable choice for furniture covers and can transform a room from cold and characterless to warm and inviting. Try the Roxburgh collection by Linwood (linwoodfabric.com).

*There are now more
contemporary carpet colours to
choose from – gentle oatmeal,
soft sage and mellow damson*

# Dining room

The handle, drape and lustre of British wool gives it a unique and timeless appeal that suits both clothing and furnishings. Plus, the UK has more sheep breeds than any other country, so there is a wide choice of colours and textures. Anta's contemporary tartan fabrics (as used in the curtains opposite) are all woven in Scotland and will bring style and warmth to a room (anta.co.uk).

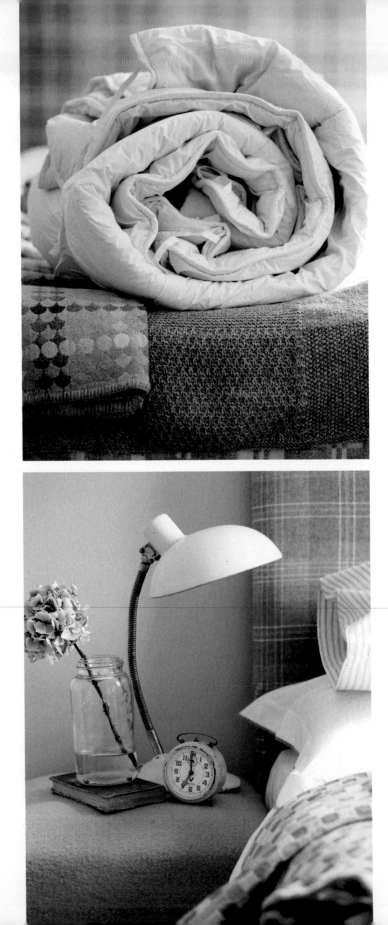

# Bedroom

Woollen cloth is a versatile material; as well as beautifully draped curtains, try using it to cover a plain headboard or for a simple upholstery project. Complete the picture with layers of blankets in traditional Welsh tapestry motifs (find a selection at melintregwynt.co.uk) or striking contemporary designs

*Wool will last longer than any other fibre and is the original eco material – annually renewable and fully biodegradable*

# THE feel-good HOME

STYLING BY **BEN KENDRICK**
ASSISTED BY **CELIA STUART-MENTETH**
PHOTOGRAPHS BY **BRENT DARBY**

*Natural* decorating schemes are calm and easy to live with but need strong textural elements for interest and warmth. Discover how to create beautiful effects by balancing the rough with the smooth in every room

*Chunky* wools, weaves and contemporary crewelwork will all bring important detail to a scheme. Here, they add extra emphasis to the more subtle, woven paisley fabric that is used on the sofa. Smooth or reflective elements, such as glassware, the Anglepoise lamp and a slate-topped table, heighten this contrast.

This pale hallway is understated and calm, with carefully chosen accessories adding textural interest. Simple brick flooring and tongue-and-groove walls offset the array of woven wicker and bamboo baskets, wooden and stone pieces, and a coir mat.

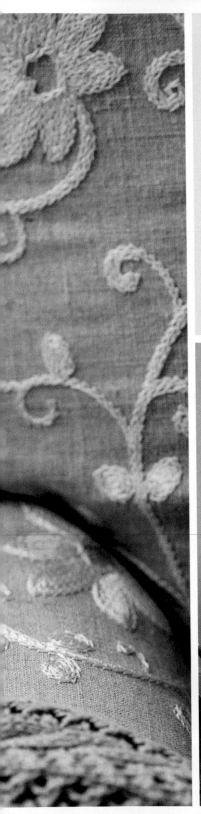

*Maximise* the effect of a neutral palette by layering simple patterns against key textures – fine embroidered cottons, decorative crewelwork, crumpled linen or loose knits. Different finishes can make a bathroom an inviting place to relax. Combine rich, polished woods with coarse weaves or soft, sensuous textiles.

# HOMES
## to inspire

*Handmade style can be introduced into any decorating look from pretty vintage to country contemporary. Take inspiration from these beautiful houses where handcrafted pieces and thrifty vintage finds take centre stage*

# Vintage style

*Retro pieces, handcrafted treasures and*

*decorative touches create a sense of*

*character and authentic country charm*

# *Rustic* renovation

*A talent for revamping and recycling has helped Beth and Travis Stevens create the home of their dreams on a shoestring in Cornwall*

WORDS BY **KATHERINE SORRELL** | PHOTOGRAPHS BY **MARK BOLTON** | STYLING BY **CAROLINE REEVES**

THIS PAGE A 1955 Aga adds to the homely feel; wild flowers from the surrounding fiaelds; vintage simplicity. OPPOSITE A cast-iron stove suits the rustic feel

It's hard to imagine Trevoole Farm as it was ten years ago – a collection of semi-derelict buildings surrounded by waist-high brambles. Today the barn, cottage and farmhouse, plus summerhouse, garden room, stable shop and potting shed, are picture perfect, each one filled with an assortment of delightful vintage, salvaged and rummaged finds. "For six months we didn't have any heating, hot water or cooking facilities in the farmhouse," Beth Stevens recalls. "We had to go to the local pub for tea and to the swimming baths for a shower."

Their adventure started in 2002, when Beth, a visual merchandiser for Laura Ashley, and her husband Travis, who has a window cleaning business, were on holiday in Cornwall. "We were living in a tiny rented cottage in Salisbury at the time and were always fantasising about moving somewhere else," Beth explains. Flicking through the local paper, they spotted an ad for an open property viewing and, on a whim, decided to go. "The 18th-century farm had been owned by the same family since 1911, and we loved the fact that nothing had changed," she explains. "It was a really special place, although the buildings were in such a bad state we couldn't look around them properly, and the three-acre field was so overgrown we didn't even realise it was there."

The purchase wasn't entirely straightforward, however, as the owner was determined only to sell Trevoole to someone he liked. "We had to be interviewed," Beth says, "but fortunately, by the end of our chat, he said we could buy it." They moved in a couple of months later and, with help from family and friends, started the long, slow ▷

process of renovation. First they divided the large granite barn into two and converted one part of it into a four-bedroom holiday cottage. Nothing had been touched since the mid-Sixties, and it took the couple three years to replace the roof and windows, sort out the plumbing and electrics, decorate and then furnish the place, all on a shoestring. Next was the farmhouse, which they rescued from an equally tumbledown condition to create another holiday let, and finally it was the turn of their own home, the smaller part of the barn, used until not long before as a milking parlour. "The ceiling was incredibly low, so Travis spent weeks digging the floor down by three feet to make it liveable," Beth recalls. "But overall our aim was for it not to be converted too much. Only the Aga and the bathroom are actually fitted – if you took the rest of our stuff out, it would still be a barn."

The Stevens' gift is not only for minimal intervention but also for ingenious recycling and repurposing, and for putting together disparate items. "Having no money was good in a way because we found an array of things from various sources and just made them all fit together," Beth says. "We turned the cow's water troughs into lights, for example, and re-used the floorboards as a partition wall. Our friend Andy made the staircase from some pitch-pine pews I bought at auction, the kitchen sink came from an old farmhouse and I bought the taps at a ▷

car-boot sale. A couple of windows even came out of a skip. I never get rid of anything – pieces wait until they find a new home. I have linen piled into cupboards and 300 china cups, for example, which come in really handy when we do our garden open days."

The buildings finished, the couple could turn their attention to the garden. "Travis spent about two years clearing brambles," Beth says. "And lots of people helped – my family, my friend Hayley came every week, visiting holidaymakers – no one seems to come here without bringing us a plant or a seedling." Now the farm has a rose walk, a herb garden, a bog garden, an orchard and a patchwork potager, as well as a variety of outbuildings and a number of animals including ducks, geese, hens, pigs, a pony and a couple of

calves to keep the grass down in summer. "We didn't know anything about having animals when we got here," Beth explains. "It just seemed like the obvious thing to do.'

"This place has required the most enormous amount of work and there are still so many more things we want to do, such as create a library in the old roundhouse. But even when we wake up and it's pouring with rain, we feel very lucky." ✒

*The gardens at Trevoole Farm are open on appointed days for the National Gardens Scheme; visit ngs.org.uk. Entry is £3; children free. The stable shop sells garden produce, preserves, cut flowers and a variety of vintage and handmade items; homemade cream teas and cakes are available in the summerhouse. For details, visit trevoolefarm.co.uk or call 01209 831243.*

OPPOSITE Old books are displayed on the stairs. THIS PAGE, CLOCKWISE FROM FAR LEFT The roll-top bath was picked up for £50; roses inspired the bedroom schemes; piles of quilts bring bursts of pattern

# IN SPLENDID
# ISOLATION

*On the windswept shores of the north-west Highlands, a
traditional white-stone croft has been transformed into the perfect
hideaway, where a sense of style and simplicity balances the
handmade craftsmanship found within*

WORDS BY **LOUISE ELLIOTT** | PHOTOGRAPHS BY **JAMES MERRELL**

Leather furniture with throws and cushions
made up in Harris tweed complete the
snug effect throughout the croft

OPPOSITE The croft is
just 50 yards from the
sea and has panoramic
views. THIS PAGE
Deep red walls and
weathered leather
furniture bring warmth
to the sitting room

To reach Callakille croft on the north-west coast of Scotland, Rosie Brown has to negotiate the infamous Bealach na Ba, or Pass of the Cattle, an old, single-track drovers' road that presents some of the most challenging driving conditions in Britain. It rises more than 2,000 feet above sea level in just five miles, zigzagging its way through the landscape in a manner that feels more alpine than Scottish. But the arduous journey is more than repaid by the beauty of the countryside – the patchwork of sea, lochs, open fields and mountains under huge, ever-changing skies – and the sheer sense of escapism.

Just 50 yards from the beach, with panoramic views of the islands of Rona, Raasay and Skye, with the Outer Hebrides looming in the distance, the croft is eight miles from the nearest village, Applecross. And its sense of remoteness is the perfect antidote to Rosie's busy life in Edinburgh, where she runs her website, Papa Stour, selling contemporary Scottish crafts and also works as a freelance photographic stylist. "A trip here restores the spirits," she says. "I really love the sense of isolation and the different way of life. All our water comes from a small burn nearby, there's no mains supply, and it has to be boiled before we can use it."

The surrounding land is still worked by families of crofters, whose sheep and cattle graze virtually up to the front door. But Rosie is no incomer – she has strong links with the area, as the croft was built by her aunt's great-uncle about 100 years ago and she often came to stay as a child, experiencing crofting life first-hand. When her aunt decided to sell the property two years ago, she was keen to take it over and maintain the family connection.

In September 2005, Rosie and her boyfriend, Ewan Findlay, began work on a six-month project to restore and repair the white-stone building. A new roof was their first ▷

OPPOSITE, TOP LEFT Layers of old wallpaper were removed to reveal the original wood panelling. BOTTOM RIGHT Rosie's style is a carefully balanced blend of vintage and modern. THIS PAGE The carved wooden table and chairs in a corner of the kitchen were a bargain from a local sale room

THIS PAGE An old cooker adds a touch of retro style to the kitchen. OPPOSITE Plain and simple kitchenware looks effective in different finishes

**Belling** Compact 4

grill  oven

priority and they wisely took the opportunity to install large Velux skylights in the two bedrooms to make the upstairs feel much lighter and larger. "Naturally, the original crofters weren't concerned about the views and the property had been built with all the windows facing east, away from the sea, as protection against the harsh weather we get up here, so it did feel very dark and rather gloomy," Rosie says. Now, light streams through the windows into the upper rooms, bouncing off the newly painted floors below and highlighting the interesting shapes of the panelled eaves.

Next, layers of wallpaper, the cracks filled with cement to keep out the wind, were peeled away to reveal the original wooden panelling beneath, patterned carpets lifted to ▷

expose the floorboards, and fire surrounds and grates uncovered. With the framework in place, Rosie set about adding her own style, a combination of vintage and modern, to every room, while also allowing the beauty of the original craftsmanship to shine through. "Most of the woodwork was done by one carpenter – you can still see where he scored his name on one of the beams in the sitting room," she says. "I wanted the croft to be a stylish retreat where we would enjoy spending time but it still had to be in tune with its surroundings."

So the dark wooden panelling has been left untouched on the stairs and in the kitchen and sitting room, but painted in contemporary shades of light grey in the bedrooms. She has introduced bolder touches, too, painting the floorboards in one of the bedrooms a deep brown that contrasts with the paler woodwork and using a shade of deep red in the sitting room: "I wanted the bedrooms to feel as light as possible but decided to make the sitting room more cosy." Weathered leather furniture and Harris tweed throws and cushions designed by Rosie complete the snug effect.

She has also kept some items left by her aunt, such as the cooker and fridge in the kitchen, which both have a retro, Fifties feel, while many of the darker pieces of wooden furniture, such as the table and chairs in the kitchen, were bought from local sale rooms. Simpler, plainer pieces were chosen for the bedrooms, with vintage quilts and painted towel rails adding just the right dose of tradition.

Rosie's next project is to put windows into the west-facing walls of the kitchen and sitting room, so she can enjoy the views from the croft even more. "There's always something to watch here – the small fishing boats setting out across the water, the lighthouses flashing in the distance, and at night we can gaze at the star-studded sky from our bed. There's nowhere quite like it." 🦆

*To rent the croft or see Rosie's online craft and design store, visit wildernesscottages.co.uk and papastour.com.*

THIS PAGE AND OPPOSITE, TOP LEFT The wooden panelling in the bedrooms has been painted a chalky pale grey to make them feel as light as possible. TOP RIGHT Rosie's love of crafts is in evidence throughout the croft

A characterful 500-year-old cottage in East Sussex provides Doris Urquhart with the perfect setting for her wonderful collections of antique china, simple rustic furniture and charming country textiles

WORDS BY **KATHERINE SORRELL** | PHOTOGRAPHS BY **CHARLIE COLMER** | STYLING BY **HESTER PAGE**

# Displaying the past

THIS PAGE Crisp, checked
fabrics offset eclectic
displays of china
and artwork. RIGHT
Doris's collection of
mochaware fills the
kitchen dresser

Doris Urquhart can't really recall when she first started to buy antiques. "I have had no formal training," she says, "but I've done it for as long as I can remember." Although she is undoubtedly knowledgeable about antiques, dates don't particularly interest her – she works by instinct. "I like shape and colour," she says. "Once I have one piece, I'll want more – I like the effect of massing things together." These tendencies are evident in her 500-year-old cottage, which is filled with English and European antiques acquired over a lifetime of collecting. It exudes comfort and calm, and manages to look uncluttered, despite the plethora of objects on every available surface.

The property wasn't in a bad state when Doris bought it, but it lacked character. The first thing she did was rip out the fitted carpets to reveal original brick and timber floors. She moved the kitchen, installing a cream Aga and a huge painted dresser, and uncovered an inglenook fireplace behind a bricked-up wall in the living room.

Decoratively, providing a simple, subtle backdrop was essential, so Doris painted ceilings, walls and woodwork with Farrow & Ball's classic neutral shade, String. At the windows, she hung only what was necessary for privacy, and eschewed rugs (despite her husband Christopher's pleas) in ▷

THIS PAGE Open shelves in the kitchen hold vintage breadboards and a mix of Scottish and salt-glazed pottery

"I like shape and colour. Once
I have one piece, I'll want more
– I like the effect of amassing
things together"

favour of bare hard floors. Introducing her selection of country and primitive furniture, along with an array of pottery, paintings, baskets and other distinctive accessories, was what finally gave the cottage life. The most impressive collection is in the kitchen, where the old dresser is laden with 19th-century English creamware and mochaware, as well as antique wooden butter stamps and a pair of magnificent Staffordshire-style china cockerels. It's an effortless display of traditional country pieces that marks Doris out as an expert collector.

Each room reveals more of her passion, from the corridor, with its Delft rack of tinware, pottery and decoy ducks, to the bathroom, where an English basin complements a Dutch mirror, a German cupboard and striped French linen towels. Very little here is modern, although in the living room a pair of armchairs – one 19th-century English, the other 18th-century French – have been re-covered in crisp, co-ordinating Ian Mankin cottons, giving them an appealing old-meets-new quality.

Ask Doris where she bought each piece and she often can't remember, and its value is definitely subordinate to her love for it. For her, it's not about money, it's not about history, it's not about knowing the exact background of every chair, bowl or basket. "I just buy what I like," she says. And it works – which is, after all, what it is all about. 🦆

OPPOSITE Old country furniture and a variety of striking paintings by Doris's daughter, artist Debbie Urquhart, create a cosy effect throughout the cottage. THIS PAGE, TOP RIGHT Antique fittings and furniture add to the character of the bathroom. BOTTOM RIGHT The bedroom is furnished with old country quilts and paintings

# The patterned house

A thrifty combination of imaginative upcycling and decorative printing has transformed a neglected farmhouse in Carmarthenshire into a colourful, comfortable family home

WORDS BY **KATHERINE SORRELL** | PHOTOGRAPHS BY **CLAIRE RICHARDSON** | STYLING BY **CAROLINE REEVES**

THIS PAGE The portrait of Caitlin Thomas, the wife of Welsh poet Dylan Thomas, was discovered in a junk shop. OPPOSITE Hand-printed cushions pick up the bright yellow of the desk in the spacious extension

THIS PAGE The 19th-century house is furnished with upcycled vintage finds. OPPOSITE In the kitchen, cupboards in a warm red contrast with the original quarry floor tiles; a hand-knitted bag; Clare with her printed fabrics

Two principles were foremost in guiding Clare Bosanquet's restoration of her west Carmarthenshire farmhouse: quality and economy. "The aim was to do it properly but cheaply, upcycling and re-using as much as possible, as well as employing traditional, environmentally friendly techniques," she explains.

It was never going to be a straightforward process, though. When art photographer Clare bought the house 11 years ago, it was a total wreck. "I didn't even have a survey as I knew it would put me off," she laughs. She had been living in East Sussex but was drawn to the beauty and remoteness of west Wales, and couldn't resist the vernacular architecture of the house – early 19th-century timber-framed, with stone walls and a slate roof – and its setting, looking out over a bucolic view of sweeping fields, and backing onto a vast coniferous forest. What she wasn't prepared for, however, was rampant dry and wet rot, endless leaks and walls that were pretty much held together only by their old flock wallpaper.

"Everything had to be done," Clare says. This included a new roof, plumbing, electrics, windows ▷

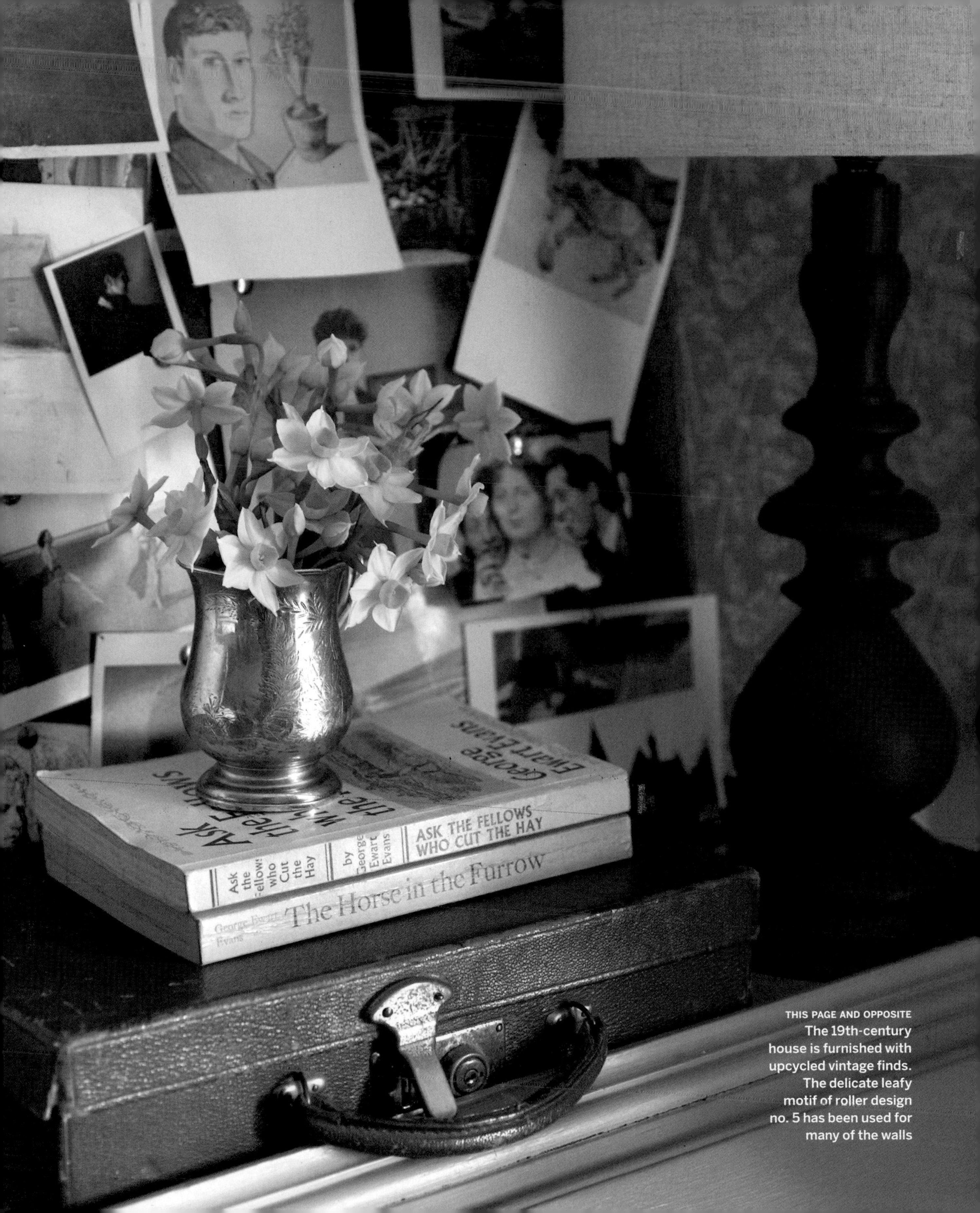
George Ewart Evans
Ask the Fellows who Cut the Hay
ASK THE FELLOWS WHO CUT THE HAY
Ask the Fellows who Cut the Hay
by George Ewart Evans
The Horse in the Furrow
George Ewart Evans

**THIS PAGE AND OPPOSITE** The 19th-century house is furnished with upcycled vintage finds. The delicate leafy motif of roller design no. 5 has been used for many of the walls

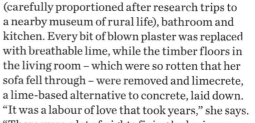

(carefully proportioned after research trips to a nearby museum of rural life), bathroom and kitchen. Every bit of blown plaster was replaced with breathable lime, while the timber floors in the living room – which were so rotten that her sofa fell through – were removed and limecrete, a lime-based alternative to concrete, laid down. "It was a labour of love that took years," she says. "There were a lot of nights fixing leaks, in my pyjamas outside in the dark. I stopped and started according to my finances, and did everything I could myself, helped by some wonderful friends. For the bits we couldn't do, I found local craftsmen who still used traditional techniques. I even learnt how to lime plaster. For a while, I had just one liveable room, so it was great when I finished the bedroom and didn't have to sleep among pots of paint any more."

Clare met her husband Sam, an ecologist, six years ago, and they finished the house together, the final job being a small extension built in 2011, when their daughter, Bea, was three years old and only days before their son Johnny was born. A timber-framed design with a corrugated tin roof and ▷

onto lime walls, and I love the look of it," she says. "I had all these wonderful walls that I didn't know what to do with, so the rollers were the perfect solution. They're very easy to use and highly addictive. I've been fine-tuning them as I've gone along, and not every room is perfect, but I love wonkiness. I also buy ex-hotel sheets on ebay as they've been washed so many times they're incredibly soft, and I then print on them and make them into tablecloths and curtains."

Clare has been inspired by Charleston, the colourful home and meeting place in East Sussex of the writers, artists and intellectuals of the Bloomsbury group, but she also loves simplicity. "Our house is pretty low-key, and we live rather quietly," she says. "With my job as a photographer, I tend to go out and be in the thick of it, and to come back here is wonderful. Also, as a soldier's daughter, I had a peripatetic childhood, so I've always wanted to have a sense of place. This is very simple but it's very much our own. I am firmly hefted to this hill and this house." ⌐

*To see Clare's range of designs, and for inspiration and instructions, visit the-painted-house.co.uk.*

walls, it is heavily insulated and extremely energy efficient. "We wanted a warm, light room where I could work while the children played," Clare says. "We all gravitate to it – it's revolutionised our lives."

Decoratively, the house came together with a combination of old family furniture and a mixture of interesting pieces that Clare rescued from various auctions, junk shops and flea markets. Chairs without seats and desks with no tops, for example, have been repaired and painted in strong colours, while throws disguise the odd bit of worn upholstery. Nothing is incredibly precious. "I'm a third-generation car-booter and an ardent upcycler," Clare explains.

Fortunately, the original quarry tiles were still in place throughout much of the ground floor, and the new lime-plastered walls provided a blank canvas. Clare used traditional Eastern European patterned paint rollers, which she first stumbled across 13 years ago in a Romanian market, to print the walls with beautiful designs that look like hand-blocked wallpaper. "You can't put wallpaper

OPPOSITE, FROM TOP Clare
also prints fabrics using
her patterned paint
rollers; Farrow & Ball's
Light Blue brings an air
of calm to the bathroom.
THIS PAGE The bedroom is
a colourful combination
of painted pieces and
vintage furniture

THIS PAGE A collection of 1940s Chalkware plates adorns the plaster-pink kitchen walls. OPPOSITE Feline friends curl up on a chair

# Full of good cheer

*Vanessa Burroughes' passion for pattern and colour brings*

*a warm, welcoming feel and striking sense of artistic beauty*

*to every corner of her 18th-century Norfolk home*

WORDS BY **LOUISE ELLIOTT** | PHOTOGRAPHS BY **CHARLIE COLMER** | STYLING BY **HESTER PAGE**

The philosophy 'less is more' is definitely not one that textile designer and printmaker Vanessa Burroughes subscribes to – plain white walls and ordered minimalism are alien concepts for her: "I can't stand any sense of emptiness – I have to be surrounded by colour and pattern, with as much as possible on display." Inside her Norfolk house, handpainted images bring the generous-sized rooms to life, collections of vintage floral china and fabrics decorate every bare space and surface, and each room is quite literally a different colour. "It's my version of what Duncan Grant and Vanessa Bell did at Charleston," she explains. In the wrong hands, this approach could easily have led to mayhem, but Vanessa has succeeded in creating a home that is as interesting and inspiring as it is cheery and welcoming.

Lying midway between Norwich and the coast, the house, originally two cottages, dates back to the 18th century and enjoys wide, open views of the flat, Norfolk countryside and the huge skies. "I came here a lot as a young girl to visit my cousins, and my great-grandfather used to live nearby," Vanessa recalls. When she decided to move out of London in 1990, it had just been renovated for rental, so she moved in – everything was painted cream and the interior felt very neutral. A few years later, however, she was able to buy the property and immediately began stamping her own style on it. "I had two young children and plenty of time on my hands in the evenings. I would put them to bed and then get painting. I liked to surprise them with colourful new pictures when they woke up in the morning."

So, in the hallway, stairs and landing, she painted a trailing design of passion flowers, datura leaves and grapevines, interspersed with birds and bamboo. "The children loved the jungly feel and I liked the idea of bringing the outside in," Vanessa explains. The painting of a flying cherub above the huge fireplace in the sitting room was inspired by post-Christmas blues: "I missed the festive images, so I decided that I would create a larger-than-life one of my own."

Vanessa feels that fear stops many people from making the most of colour ▷

OPPOSITE, BELOW LEFT Orangey-pink walls echo the hues of upholstery in the sitting room. TOP RIGHT Kitchen cupboards and a plate rack are painted in Farrow & Ball's Ballroom Blue. THIS PAGE The house has gradually become a canvas for Vanessa's artistic talents

THIS PAGE The blue Aga was the starting point in the colourful kitchen. OPPOSITE Fresh blooms from the garden are wrapped in floral paper designed by Vanessa

in their home. Her experience as a textile designer, at one point working for GP & J Baker and Liberty, taught her how to be more adventurous: "I'm happy to experiment and not afraid of making mistakes. I chalk out a rough design and then free paint with emulsion – if you go wrong, you can always go over it."

The kitchen is the perfect example of how she is able to combine different shades in an artistic way, the starting point for the whole scheme being the blue Aga she was allowed to specify when she first began renting the house. Plaster-pink walls, salvaged black and red floor pamments, a red Smeg fridge and sky-blue cupboards bring the room to life, their colours picked up in the vintage ceramics, including her much-loved 1940s Chalkware, that fill shelves and decorate walls. Vanessa is a passionate collector of old fabrics and china, and her magpie instincts

mean she is always introducing new pieces into the house. "It doesn't matter if they are broken or torn, the colours and patterns help spark off new ideas and arrangements," she says. Country house sales, bric-a-brac shops, local field sales and the auction house, Keys, in Aylsham, are all favourite hunting grounds.

Vanessa doesn't like rooms to stand still, and versatile touches mean fresh ideas can be easily introduced. The curtain at the kitchen window, for example, is just a piece of fabric wrapped around a pole and can be changed on a whim. Windows in the sitting room are left bare in summer to flood the room with light, but hung with thick curtains in winter to create a warm, cosy feel.

Beautiful prints by Vanessa, many inspired by old china and textiles, introduce further layers of colour and pattern, as do her tapestry cushions

and quilts made from an assortment of 1950s fabrics. "When my partner Paul goes to other people's houses, he says they look as though they've been burgled, as everything feels so bare compared with here!" she laughs. This exuberant quality suits a house that is now home to her two children, three step-children, seven cats, three dogs and around 30 bantams.

Together with lecturing part-time in textiles, Vanessa also runs a shop, Verandah, in Norwich, with four other local artists who make and design an eclectic range of prints, textiles, ceramics, jewellery, wrapping papers and cards. "As well as my vintage collections, I also have lots of their pieces in the house but we may have to start extending if I'm going to fit everything in..." ➴

*Verandah, 85 Upper St Giles, Norwich (01603 666137; verandah-norwich.co.uk).*

Vanessa's magpie instincts mean she is
always introducing new decorative pieces

# Coastal charm

*Choose furniture made from sunbleached*

*driftwood, jaunty striped fabrics and a palette*

*that echoes the shades of the sea*

# The handcrafted home

The grains, colours and textures of reclaimed wood give character and contemporary style to a coastal retreat created from a neglected house above a Cornish cove

WORDS BY **LOUISE ELLIOTT** | PHOTOGRAPHS BY **CHARLIE COLMER**
STYLING BY **HESTER PAGE**

"I go down to the beach every day, no matter the weather, looking for interesting pieces of wood that I can use in the house"

After living in Cornwall for 26 years, most recently running her own organic farm, Barbara Mills was more than keen to realise her long-held dream of waking up to a sea view. "I'd always lived inland," she says, "but I'm a complete beach addict and came to this cove to hunt for driftwood and firewood – I loved the sense of peace and seclusion, with the green hills rising gently behind, the river to one side and the Atlantic stretching in front as far as the eye can see. I used to gaze up at this house and think how forlorn and neglected it looked. When it came up for sale early in 2006, I knew I could do something with it, no matter how rundown it was. I was just entranced by the location, and the idea of having my own path from the garden down to the sea below was irresistible."

Standing above Wanson Mouth cove on the rugged north Cornish coast near Bude, the house had been built from bricks made on the beach to create cheap housing during the Second World War. Although the outside walls had been recently replaced, the inside remained a rabbit warren of dark, cramped rooms with only a few small windows that ▷

**FROM FAR BOTTOM LEFT** Utensils hang from a piece of driftwood; salvaged timber and granite in the kitchen reflect the colours of the beach; Barbara loves the creative inspiration that living by the sea gives her

almost obscured the beautiful seascape outside. "The condition was so bad that I virtually had to rebuild the inside – all the floor joists and roof beams have been replaced, and it's been totally rewired and replumbed," Barbara explains. Partitions were knocked down and ceilings raised to create a more spacious, open-plan layout consisting of a large kitchen-diner, huge sitting area and hallway, and three bedrooms, with French doors leading onto tiered, decked terraces. Walls were painted a clean white and the new wooden floors limewaxed to give a pale, bleached effect. "It felt big, bright and sunny, like a contemporary beach house," she says, "but it was basically a plain shell. I still wanted the look to be essentially quite simple, yet I needed to add character for it to feel like a home."

Today, it is the grains, colours and textures of wood that bring warmth to the house and introduce a sense of drama and impact. Much of it is driftwood collected by Barbara from the cove ("I'm down

on the beach every day, no matter the weather, looking for interesting finds, and often with my horse, Chequer") or foraged pieces from local timber and salvage yards ("I'm passionate about the environment and using reclaimed materials"). So, in her bedroom, a large, chunky length of wood unearthed from a nearby saw mill has been fashioned into a striking, organically curved table, a lump of driftwood topped with a coil of rope makes an interesting lamp base, while an old cable reel picked up from the beach has become an individual surround for a mirror. Plain white cotton curtains at the large windows are tied back with small, curved pieces of driftwood linked together. "I love the idea of making something out of nothing and thinking of new artistic ways with raw materials," Barbara says, another case in point being the sculptural candle holder in the dining room she created from a branched piece of driftwood.

Kitchen cupboards were made from wood rescued from the wreck of the ▷

FROM TOP LEFT Barbara has a collection of horse paintings; Atlantic waves roll into the cove; a decked terrace from the dining room allows her to enjoy the stunning sea views at all times of day

Shades of the sea
are further reflected
in Barbara's choice
of fabrics, all with
a contemporary and
cool feel

*Kodima,* which went aground on Whitsand Bay in 2001 – Barbara collected some of it herself and bought the rest from the salvors. A curly piece of driftwood hung below the cupboards is used for hanging utensils and adds an unusual decorative touch. Granite worktops and tiles inset with pebbles echo the materials and colours of the shoreline. "I also wanted something that would look quite dramatic against the pale walls and floors," Barbara adds.

Shades of the sea are further reflected in Barbara's choice of fabrics, but the feel is cool and contemporary rather than jolly and jaunty – in her bedroom, a fine blue-and-white striped material covers the sofa rescued from a skip, its colour turned to slate in the strong sunlight, and cobalt blue linen and bleached calico cushions cover her large bed crafted from lengths of driftwood.

With its own balcony and double set of French doors, the bedroom is Barbara's favourite room in the house she has skilfully transformed from an ugly 1930s design into a contemporary coastal retreat: "I love to fall asleep with the doors open and hear the waves crashing on the beach. So even at night I'm reminded that I finally have my house with a sea view." ⌁

LEFT In the dining room, sleek chairs contrast with the expanse of natural wood. A chunky table created from salvaged timber is evidence of Barbara's talent for using reclaimed materials

# Seaside simplicity

*Ginny Morgan's inspiring family home on Guernsey perfectly demonstrates her eye for the beautiful and the unusual*

WORDS BY **CAROLINE ATKINS**
PHOTOGRAPHS **BY CLAIRE RICHARDSON**
STYLING BY **BEN KENDRICK**

THIS PAGE Glass, shells, graphic letters and Ginny's handmade calico dolls form still-life arrangements. OPPOSITE Ginny sews all her own cushions from vintage fabrics

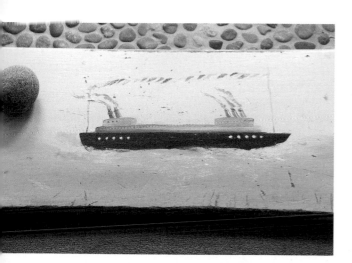

T here's an air of suspended celebration about Ginny Morgan's Guernsey home. The coloured bunting still hangs across the kitchen where it was strung for someone's birthday and never taken down. Little dishes of bright sea-washed 'treasure' sit on tables and mantelpieces. And the grey slate roof is trimmed with decorative barge-boarding like the icing of a cake. Yet beneath all this gaiety, the simple, white-painted rooms are as cool and calm as one of the pebbles Ginny collects from the beach three miles away.

It's 15 years now since Ginny and her husband, Jason, bought the late-Victorian villa. Guernsey-born, they had re-met while working in London, where Jason was a lawyer and Ginny had trained as an illustrator at Central Saint Martins. "But every time I came home I felt a real pull," she says. So they moved back in 1992 and married on the island, living in a flat above her family's cake shop – and then in Jason's parents' barn – until they found this place, which was, Ginny says, 'perfect'.

But although perfect from an artistic point of view, it wasn't hugely practical for a young couple with a small child. Their son Hugo was two when they bought it, and they spent an initial six months, with him in tow, working on it in the evenings and at weekends to make it habitable. Very dilapidated, it had been divided into two flats by the previous owners. "The first thing we did," Ginny remembers, "was to knock down a partitioning wall that butted right up to the banisters to divide the upper and lower flats." Having opened up the beautifully proportioned hall, they worked room by room to ▷

The simple white
backdrop is brought
to life by interesting
artistic details

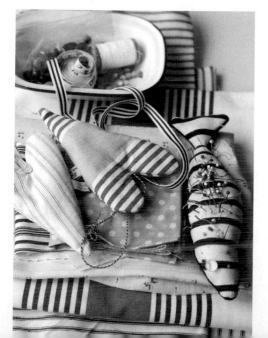

strip old paper, replaster the walls, replace plastic windows with traditional wooden sashes, and turn it back into a single two-bedroom house. By the time they had restored it to its Victorian self, they knew they were expecting twins. Isabelle and Theo were born in 1995, so for their first couple of years in the house all three children bunked in together, dormitory-style. Since then, the Morgans have adapted as they've needed to, extending outwards downstairs to give them a big family kitchen, a small sitting room and a children's room that runs from front to back across one side. They then built on top of the ground-floor extension and into the roof, to accommodate a fourth child, Edmund, and provide an extra attic bathroom from which you can just see the sea in the distance.

The simple white backdrop is brought to life with touches of other colours (mostly Farrow & Ball's Skylight blue) and interesting artistic details. ▷

OPPOSITE Blue and white keeps the mood fresh and light in the children's room. THIS PAGE, FROM ABOVE Coastal-themed accessories on a mantelpiece; work in progress in Ginny's studio

Ginny's illustrator's eye will always light on the beautiful and enjoy the unusual. She instinctively collects source material wherever she goes – old fabrics from markets, stamps from envelopes, stones from the beach and snatches of elegant lettering, such as the printed paper bag from the Musée D'Orsay in Paris that stands propped on a sitting-room shelf.

Ginny's studio overlooks the garden and is crammed with fragments and ideas, bolts of fabric and paper, and the scrapbooks in which she files anything that inspires her – including the torn-out page from *Country Living* where she spotted Plain English kitchens, the company who made the pale painted cabinets now festooned with bunting.

Apart from making all her own cushions and curtains, she also sells little calico sailors and dolls (under the name of EDITH, an acronym of her children's initials) in local shops in St Peter Port. Several of these sit on her own shelves, alongside the shells, feathers and dried sea anemones that turn each surface into something like one of those beautifully still, stylised nature-table paintings by Mary Fedden.

It's the sort of house where everyone tends to congregate in the kitchen, but the garden is also coming into its own. Nothing but greenhouses and land when they first arrived, it's now filled with raspberry bushes and fruit trees. They also planted an oak for each of the children and the alders are fast gaining height: "We can now sling hammocks between them," Ginny says. "It's wonderful to feel so rooted in a home." 🦆

# Ancient
# & modern

*Past and present can be combined to*

*striking effect when a sense of handmade*

*simplicity unites the look*

# In *perfect* harmony

Contemporary country style complements the original features of a 16th-century farmhouse in Sussex, resulting in a family home full of character

WORDS AND STYLING BY **GABI TUBBS** | PHOTOGRAPHS BY **JODY STEWART**

THIS PAGE The oak kitchen; vintage linen cushions. OPPOSITE Upholstered furniture creates an understated country look

When Paul and Tamsin Clarke decided it was time for them to move out of London, they spent a year searching for a new home before finally discovering a perfect patch of countryside in East Sussex that was way beyond their expectations – a place where they could enjoy glorious scenery and stunning coastline as well as the occasional fix of urban life.

Just a few miles south of Lewes, tucked away in the lee of a hill at the foot of the South Downs, lies the unspoilt village of Kingston: "It was exactly what we were looking for," Tamsin recalls. "It had all the elements of the quintessential English village – a pub housed in two 14th-century cottages, a Norman church, a village hall and a primary school." The centre, known as The Street, also had a small number of listed cottages with neat gardens hidden behind ivy-clad flint walls and filled with a glorious profusion of country flowers and shrubs from spring to autumn. "The first house we looked at

in the village slipped through our fingers and we were about to delay our move for another year, then we discovered this 16th-century farmhouse and were determined to make it our home," Tamsin explains.

Originally one cottage, with another added at a later stage, the farmhouse is unpretentious but full of character: walls are crooked, floors uneven, including the beautiful original red-brick flooring in the narrow hallway. And, despite its age, the property needed very little structural work, apart from re-pointing at the front, which was a definite attraction.

It wasn't just the house that captivated the couple, though. Paul fell in love with the traditional cottage garden with its lavender-flanked path, flowering shrubs, old roses and fruit trees. The excitement at the sight of a small vegetable plot, a stretch of lawn for their young son Zach to play on and a secluded corner for alfresco meals, as well as a ruined bakery with its brick oven intact, swept away any doubts they might have had about leaving London. From ▷

In the dining room, a homely but modern edge has been created with a combination of metal, wood and glass

Throughout the house, muted tones and natural
materials are used alongside ancient and modern pieces

the outset, Tamsin and Paul knew they
wanted to create an interior with a homely
but modern edge rather than traditional
English cottage style. Every room had been
whitewashed, creating a blank canvas, which
meant they could start from scratch and
make the house their own. They decided
to buy only furniture and accessories they
were really taken with and were prepared
to wait for the right pieces, so were delighted
to discover Flint, a lifestyle and homeware
store in Lewes, where they always found the
perfect item. To speed up the process, they
sought advice from the owners, Heidi Francis
and her mother Julia, who recommended
subtle paint colours and complementary
fabrics, and found and upholstered furniture,
to create an understated country look.
Today, muted tones and natural materials
sit alongside ancient and modern pieces,
particularly noticeable in the dining room,

where contemporary metal chairs surround
a 17th-century round wooden table bought
at an auction house and then stripped
and re-varnished. Interest is added to the
calming palette with different textures,
such as heavy curtains in the sitting room
that keep it cosy on chilly evenings, a
cow-hide rug in the dining room and
weathered vintage furniture throughout.

Once the interior was finished, they could
turn their attention to the garden. Paul
cleared a spot for the beehive and bees he
ordered and the couple are hoping for their
first honey this year. The family are now
well and truly part of the village. Zach is
at the small village school, which is within
walking distance of the farmhouse, and their
new neighbours and friends are always
popping in for a cup of tea or glass of wine.
Life in the country is proving to be everything
they had hoped for – and more. ◀

LEFT The iron chapel is Grade II listed. THIS PAGE Nick made the kitchen units using leftover tiles and recycled zinc

# Chapel *of* DREAMS

*Salvaged pieces have been imaginatively repurposed inside craftsman Nick Kenny's Victorian corrugated-iron chapel in the historic port of Faversham in Kent*

WORDS BY **CAROLINE ATKINS** | PHOTOGRAPHS BY **EMMA LEE** | STYLING BY **BEN KENDRICK**

Nick Kenny had no intention of buying a chapel when he began looking for a property to renovate a few years ago, but he was definitely looking for somewhere unusual where he could use his skills as a craftsman to maximum effect. "I was trying to buy a foundry in Ramsgate at the time," he recalls. "I'd just lost out on that when my brother-in-law heard about this place. It wasn't being advertised – quite a few people have since told me they'd have bought it if they'd known it was for sale – and he had heard about it by word of mouth. I fell head over heels in love with the building – and ignored the thought of how much it might cost to make it habitable."

The chapel was originally a Church of England building, paid for by the community and bought flat-packed from a catalogue (William Cooper, in London's Old Kent Road). "Hundreds of these places were put up during the late 1800s," Nick explains. "You could pay extra for features like porches, steeples and stained glass, depending on how elaborate you wanted it to be. Mine still has its original wrought-iron finials along the ridge of the roof, decorative bargeboards with patterns cut into the cedar, and Alpha and Omega designs worked into the glass of the altar window." The building also used to have a bell in the tower, but when the chapel was deconsecrated in 1962, it was given to another church. Latterly, it has been used for all sorts of things, including a scout hut and, most recently, a joinery.

The first obstacle Nick encountered was changing the building's status to a domestic dwelling, but fortunately the local council conservation officer liked the idea of the chapel being inhabited by some kind of artist and allowed Nick the initial use of a 'section' of the building – which has expanded over time: "The rest of the space is considered empty as it ▷

contains pieces of furniture I'm adapting for my projects, and so not habitable."

The chapel was still full of timber and old joinery machinery when Nick first moved in, so clearing this away had to be given priority, along with repairing the badly damaged floor. For 18 months, he managed with little more than cold running water, a kettle, a sink unit and a small water heater, while he installed a shower and built the kitchen – both imaginatively repurposed from scrap and salvage.

Remarkably, every element of the simple but stylish interior he has created was 'found' and reworked by hand. "I love trawling around salvage yards," Nick says. "And in summer, I work my way round a map of the *vides greniers* in France – sort of clearance sales – which last right through to September. And there are some good car-boot sales in this area, too – I know which ones to go to. The spiral staircase up to the sleeping platform

(a sort of 'floating' mezzanine level above the kitchen) came from ebay – it's actually an old external fire escape – and the green light fittings were a job lot – 15 or 20 of them – from a local sale."

The whole project proves just how much can be achieved on a pretty tight budget. The glass-fronted wall cabinet in the kitchen was picked up for £25 from an auction, while the marble worktop was rescued from a job where it was being thrown out, and smaller pieces have been cut down from Victorian washstands. Nick has a horror of standard, fitted units and loves using Paris roof zinc (from the city's scrapyards) to bring individual detail to cupboard doors and end pieces: "I prefer the underside, which is marked with interesting patterns from where the metal came into contact with the timber." In both the kitchen and bathroom, old salvaged tiles have been used alongside new ones to create

an interesting effect. "I like to be able to see the signs of repairs," he says.

A cool, contemporary palette of whites and blue-greys has been used throughout, which is perfectly in keeping with the functional simplicity and handmade character of the space. Woodwork around the Gothic arched windows and doors has been highlighted to emphasise their architectural beauty, and darker grey used on the rafters that soar above.

There are still a few projects on Nick's to-do list but that's all part of the fun. "Some of the windows don't open, and I must improve the insulation. You need a sense of humour to take on a place like this – you just have to love it and appreciate all its quirkiness. I feel rather like I'm a care worker for an inanimate object. But I'm at home here. It's been revalued at about three times what I paid for it, and lots of people have asked for first refusal if I ever sell – but I won't." ◄

OPPOSITE AND THIS PAGE Lots of handcrafted details, such as stencilled wording on walls, and upholstered chairs, can be seen in the chapel

STYLING BY **HESTER PAGE**
WORDS BY **CAROLINE ATKINS**
PHOTOGRAPHS BY **JAMES MERRELL**

# Recycled &
# reclaimed

*Boonshill Farm has
the appearance of
the quintessential
Sussex farmhouse. Its interior, however, has been transformed
by an inspiring and idiosyncratic use of reclaimed materials to
create a home of weathered style and distinctive character*

Beams, brickwork and oak
floorboards are exposed so the
original surfaces provide their
own character

THIS PAGE Hand-sewn loose covers are used
on a sofa, while a raft of old china
lines a pantry wall. OPPOSITE Old and new
merge beautifully in the kitchen

Romney Marsh has a wild beauty and an adventurous past: it's a place of sheep, smugglers and of fierce storms that have, over the centuries, lashed its coastline and flooded its pastures. In this sometimes bleak landscape, working farmland is dotted with isolated houses, and it is in one of these, near the village of Iden, not far from Rye, that garden designer Lisette Pleasance has made a home for herself – and for B&B guests who want to enjoy her garden-grown food and quietly idiosyncratic furnishings.

Her 18th-century farmhouse, reached by a cinder track, has glimpses of the sea beyond its 14 acres of fields, and conveys instant tranquillity. Enchanted by its weatherboarding and Kent peg tiles, all mellowed and lichen-clad, Lisette knew she had found the perfect place to pursue her dream of self-sufficiency.

Hers has been a life of contrasts, growing up in India where her father worked, but going to boarding school in Kent; reading John Seymour's *Complete Book of Self-Sufficiency* at 18, then coming back to London and working as a potter before switching to garden design. Yet the last few years seem to have imposed their own order, drawing her away from the London gardens where she worked during the 1980s and 1990s, first to the west London village of Petersham, where she managed Petersham Nurseries, and finally down to the Sussex coast, an area familiar from childhood holidays.

Boonshill Farm itself has the neat proportions of a child's drawing. Inside, though, Lisette and her partner, Mick Shaw, have worked with the natural lines of the building to open up its space and reflect its age. Ceilings have been taken down so you can see into the rafters; beams, brickwork and oak floorboards exposed so the original surfaces provide their own character. In keeping with the adventurous ▷

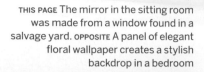
THIS PAGE The mirror in the sitting room was made from a window found in a salvage yard. OPPOSITE A panel of elegant floral wallpaper creates a stylish backdrop in a bedroom

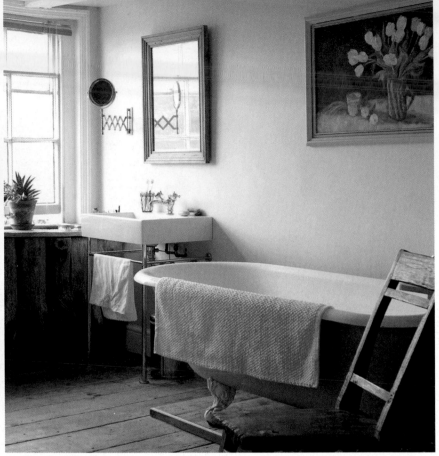

spirit of the marsh, they have introduced sleek industrial kitchen units alongside the old Aga. But the real challenge Lisette and Mick set themselves, here and in the rest of the house – was to recycle as much as possible. "Mick can turn his hand to making almost anything, and we're always rummaging around in salvage yards," Lisette says. "I love the look of reclaimed wood – if you choose the right pieces, you find wonderful marks left from nails and joints."

Lisette's plan is for B&B guests to feel as much at home here as she does. The brick-floored dining room, its chunky table made by Mick from 17th-century oak floorboards, and the sunlit sitting room, where a grandfather clock ticks in one corner, both have inglenook fireplaces. Upstairs, the three bedrooms finished so far (two for guests) have their own bathrooms and are furnished with the same distinctive style and

recycling ingenuity as the living rooms. Reclaimed wrought-iron garden gates make striking decorative bedheads, and the wooden bed frame in the main bedroom was built from old banisters, with newel posts for the corners.

As for the garden, Lisette has taken to self-sufficiency as though by instinct. Her meadows of poppies, cornflowers and daisies have encouraged flocks of butterflies and hummingbird moths in their hundreds. A new orchard has added mulberries, cherries, almonds and walnuts to the existing supplies of plums, apples and pears. Her own pigs and chickens provide bacon and eggs for guests' breakfasts, and the produce from the vegetable garden is plentiful. "There's a lifetime's work here," Lisette admits. But, then, she already feels as though she has lived here all her life. ↵

*Double B&B at Boonshill Farm costs from £90; call 01797 280533 or see boonshillfarm.co.uk for details.*

THIS PAGE Stylish simplicity in the kitchen with its rustic enamelware and Shaker-style freestanding cupboards. OPPOSITE White walls lighten the landing; exposed brick and stone bring natural beauty to the garden room

BREAD

# A sense *of* serenity

*A palette of pure, intense whites, softened with gentle greens, stripped wood and simple, natural accessories, creates a feeling of peace, tranquillity and space inside Maddie Thornhill's beautiful Sussex home*

WORDS AND STYLING BY **GABI TUBBS** | PHOTOGRAPHS BY **CAROLINE ARBER**

It was quite a wrench for garden photographer Maddie Thornhill to leave her beautiful five-storey Georgian house on Worthing seafront in West Sussex, but the size and responsibility of it were becoming a worry. "When the winter storms came, I often thought the roof would blow away completely!" Maddie recalls. Planning to downscale to a smaller house in the same county, she was drawn to the market town of Arundel with its magnificent castle. Having viewed more than 25 properties, she had almost given up hope when a friend rang to tell her that The Garden House, a terraced cottage just off the High Street, had come up for sale and advised her to view it quickly. Maddie immediately felt sure that she and her daughter Cassie would be happy here: "I decided to make my offer before anyone else had a chance."

Charming as it was, the house still needed plenty of love and attention to bring it alive. The starting point was a complete re-decoration from top to bottom, which Maddie undertook herself. Starting with the ceilings, and using her old favourite, Egyptian Cotton by Dulux, she painted the dark wood-stained beams to lighten the mood. Little ▷

THIS PAGE White upholstery, walls and curtains offset displays of old agricultural tools and salvaged ironwork in the sitting room, with galvanised planters and zinc pieces introducing a contemporary element

THIS PAGE The cabin bed in the attic. OPPOSITE, FROM LEFT A mass of freshly cut lilac in a tall galvanised bucket forms a beautiful display; a wisteria canopy creates the perfect setting for lazy lunches in the garden

decision-making was required for the walls as Maddie rarely wavers from white, the more brilliant and more intense the better. But touches of colour have been used for the woodwork, which is painted in varying subtle shades of blue and green.

She sensibly postponed delivery of most of the furniture until all the renovation work had been completed. For two months, they survived with just two beds, two bedside lights, a small table and two chairs while a complete electrical rewiring, boiler replacement and kitchen re-fit took place. A carpenter friend helped to hang traditional ledge-and-brace stripped doors in all the rooms and installed the Shaker-style cupboards in the kitchen. He also made the cabin bed in the attic bedroom to Maddie's design, with plenty of storage space underneath.

Once the basic renovations were completed, carpets laid and the furniture in place, Maddie and Cassie were finally able to relax, although it wasn't long before Maddie began planning how she could transform the damp and dingy cellar into a Mediterranean garden room. Tons of rubble and earth were dug out, exterior steps laid and the floor dropped by 18 inches. Furniture is kept simple with an old metal café-style table and chairs, while stone steps rise straight into the sitting room and help integrate the space with the rest of the house.

Today, the property feels like a sizeable country cottage rather than a terraced house in town. The abundance of white increases the feeling of space, with areas of colour echoing the calm shades of the garden. Furniture, rugs and china have a simple, natural feel with galvanised metal pieces adding to the sense of light. "As a photographer, light is important to me," Maddie says. "Here, I've used it to create a feeling of peace. And that, above all, is what every home should offer." 🦆

*See Maddie's photographs at maddiethornhill.com.*

# Country contemporary

*Simple pieces of traditional rustic*

*furniture fit perfectly with a pared-back*

*look and chalky off-white hues*

# Labour *of* LOVE

A patient approach and an ability to turn his hand
to traditional skills has enabled a sculptor and his family to
restore a Cornish farmhouse with sensitivity and style

WORDS BY **SUE GILKES** | PHOTOGRAPHS BY **POLLY WREFORD** | STYLING BY **JULIA BIRD**

THIS PAGE AND OPPOSITE Distinctive
early works in canvas, twigs and
twine sit perfectly with the earthy,
textured look of the old
longhouse. The ceilings of all the
rooms upstairs were removed,
exposing the ancient beams and
increasing the sense of space

"I can only take on one really major project in my lifetime," declared William Peers on seeing Moreton Mill for the first time, excited yet a little daunted by the thought that this might be it. On the Cornish side of the River Tamar, the 400-year-old longhouse was in a run-down state but it also had several dilapidated barns and outbuildings with potential studio space for William, who is a sculptor, plus 14 acres of land. If his wife Sophie thought he was being a little melodramatic at the time, ten years on she appreciates the significance of his words. The couple were renting nearby – William knew the area, as he had spent several summers working there and it appealed to Sophie because it reminded her of Ireland, where she grew up. "Cornwall feels more Celtic than other parts of England," she explains.

Fitting in work around William's shows and the arrival of three children, as well as Sophie's job as deputy editor of the ecology magazine *Resurgence*, they have gradually rebuilt the house themselves, with William learning traditional skills where needed. Though the farmhouse's interior had not been touched for 50 years, the original cob walls had been covered with Victorian lathe and plaster, creating a series of

small, box-like rooms. When William took this down, it greatly increased the size of the rooms but also revealed huge holes in the cob behind. Luckily, the damage wasn't structural – the ancient walls were two-foot thick in some places – but they did need to be repaired.

So William taught himself to work with cob, in the process discovering old doorways and fireplaces that had been walled over: but the most fascinating items were hidden in the cob itself. It had been the custom, in more superstitious times when these ancient houses were being built, to place personal items in the corners of rooms, in the belief that they would distract any mischievous spirits entering the house. William found a tiny leather child's shoe, old coins, a comb made of bone and round stones like marbles during the restoration. Sophie hopes one day to display their 'cob ephemera': in the meantime, they've continued the tradition by replacing anything removed from the cob with old personal items of their own. Used to

working with his hands in wood, stone and other natural materials, William is immensely practical and likes a challenge. So when they needed terracotta tiles for the kitchen floor, he decided to make them – a lengthy process that involved digging and purifying the clay, making a mould and building a huge kiln outside to fire the tiles. "By doing it yourself, you learn so much about the materials and it becomes an interesting project in itself," Sophie says.

William also learnt how to cobble, and even to thatch when the round cob house he built for their donkeys needed a roof – the only drawback being that its residents found it made a delicious snack. He is an equally accomplished roofer, scouring the area for suitable second-hand 'rag' slates. Endlessly sourcing items for the house, he has been delighted with the treasures yielded by local reclamation yards. All the vintage toilets and basins at Moreton Mill came from the dump nearby, with none costing more than £10, and ▷

"We like the idea of using natural
materials and living very simply
with few things"

OPPOSITE The wide floorboards upstairs were created from the broad trunks of Shropshire oak trees. THIS PAGE, FROM RIGHT William at work; colourful ethnic textiles brighten the main bedroom; Miskin the cat on a bench of reclaimed wood

their splendid Victorian roll-top bath was spotted in a friend's farmyard filled with baler twine.

William has a keen eye for salvageable bits and pieces, stashing 'found objects' and materials in their old barns – and because he has the skills and the tools, he eventually always finds a way to use them in the house, transforming odd blocks of slate into rough-hewn splashbacks for sinks, for example.

Sophie has similar acquisitive tendencies. "I have a luggage addiction," she admits, but she justifies her collection of vintage trunks and old leather suitcases picked up in flea markets and charity shops by using them to store everything from paperwork to the children's toys. She is especially fond of those covered in evocative labels from long-forgotten journeys around the globe: "They have had wonderful lives – they've got soul," she enthuses. "I like things that have a history to them."

This was a large part of the appeal of Moreton Mill and why she and William felt they didn't wish to impose a particular style on the house. Sophie loves the way it has developed organically over the years with William doing the structural work while she has focused on the interior. A mix of quirky, salvaged-wood furniture, junk-shop finds and old kilims has created an earthy, rustic look that works well with William's abstract textural stone pieces, which hang from walls or rest on broad windowsills throughout the house, giving it a very grounded feel. And the traditional pale limewashed cob walls provide the perfect backdrop. "We like the idea of using natural materials and living very simply with few things," she explains.

This philosophy certainly seems in tune with Moreton Mill, which has proved itself worthy of their thoughtful treatment in its gradual metamorphosis from a neglected wreck to a warm, welcoming home. *William's work can be seen at williampeers.com and at the John Martin Gallery in London (020 7499 1314; jmlondon.com).*

# PALE & interesting

Fran Switherns' passion for old buildings and pieces from the past has transformed a crumbling coach house into a stylish and welcoming home with a history

WORDS BY **HEATHER GRATTON** | PHOTOGRAPHS BY **RACHEL WHITING**
STYLING BY **FRANCINE KAY**

Everything in the tiny coach
house has been kept pared
back to preserve the integrity
of the original building

"If there's one thing I love, it's a challenge, so when I stepped into that dark space with its bare brick walls, old timbers and block floor, I just couldn't resist – I was smitten," Fran Switherns says, explaining why she decided to buy the run-down coach house that is now her inviting, light-filled home in East Sussex.

Fran had been living in the countryside but then her marriage broke up. "I wanted to find a new life and it made sense for me to move nearer to my family and friends in Hove." When her sister spotted the coach house, after only a week of searching, everything seemed to fall into place. Surrounded by mature trees and with a rustic feel, it offered a perfect solution to Fran's dilemma: it was centrally located but quiet, tucked out of view behind a terrace of beautiful Victorian houses, within easy reach of the Sussex Downs and only a stone's throw from the beach.

As an interior designer, Fran understood the scale of work required but was confident she could transform the property: "I love barns and outhouses with their character and atmosphere." Her passion for these old buildings, stemming from a rural childhood, is evident throughout the conversion as she was determined to preserve its integrity by salvaging original materials wherever possible. Fortunately, Fran found a local builder who shared her passion for recycling.

Built over 100 years ago to house the horses and a stable boy for the adjoining property, the coach house was one of the last remaining in the area. It consisted of two stable blocks on the ground floor with a hayloft on the first floor and was being used as a garage and storage place, but Fran was able to see beyond the old motorbikes and spare parts. Much of the interior structure had to be ripped out. "I found it heartbreaking seeing all this history disappearing," Fran confesses, "but I ended up storing everything that I removed – floorboards, stable doors and flooring – in ▷

"I chose the ceramic floor tiles not only for their pattern and colour but also because I could clean them easily – important with a dog and chickens"

the hope that I could use most of it again." Planning restrictions had to be considered, so Fran was faced with some difficult decisions. The windows on the ground floor were kept, but building regulations dictated the installation of secondary glazing. She made sure this didn't detract from the original style, and, once the ceiling was lowered, the possibilities opened up.

The first job was to reinstate the floorboards upstairs and replace rotten ones with reclaimed boards. Downstairs, it wasn't so easy. "I wanted to keep the original stable-block flooring but it wasn't practical," Fran remembers. "It was also very patchy, with broken pieces that were beyond repair. I ended up selling it all on ebay and using the money to buy these beautiful ceramic floor tiles instead. I chose them not only for their pattern and colour but also because I could clean them easily – an important consideration with a dog and chickens wandering in and out."

Once the basic structure was in place, the interior began to take shape. "I pared back everything to allow the feel of the building to come through," Fran says. "I used the original bricks to build a dividing wall in the bedroom, making an ideal space for a shower room. And, ▷

OPPOSITE In the living room, originally the stable block, a leather sofa and antlers create a Scandinavian look. THIS PAGE Handcrated baskets are used as handy storage

THIS PAGE Striped
African rugs and old
wooden furniture
add interest to the
open-plan living area

To maximise the sense of space,
the walls and woodwork are
painted white throughout

THIS PAGE The traditional
ledge-and-brace doors
were made from
reclaimed wood.
OPPOSITE Organic
fabrics and vintage
accessories add to the
handcrafted theme

Nearly everything was salvaged from the building or found at reclamation yards

once the roof had been insulated, we installed beams to create a more authentic feel."

Fran commissioned traditional ledge-and-brace doors, made from reclaimed wood and Suffolk ironmongery, to continue the rustic theme. And in the living area she has left the plaster walls unpainted, which, together with the new woodburning stove, create a wonderfully warm atmosphere. Upstairs is light and airy despite being small. The walls and woodwork are painted white throughout to maximise the sense of space, and an eclectic mix of wooden furniture lends a homespun charm. Apart from the appliances, everything was salvaged from the building or found at reclamation yards. "I was determined not to buy anything off the shelf," Fran explains, confessing to her passion for scouring antiques shops and fairs in her search for furniture – pieces with patina and a history. "It feels like a country cottage, although I'm in a town. I really do have the best of both worlds."

The conversion is complete but, for Fran, this is just the beginning of another project. Inspired by designing and furnishing the coach house, she has set herself a new challenge and started a business. Her home becomes a pop-up shop where everything is sold, from the furniture to the ceramic tiles. "It is hard to part with pieces I love, but the fun is sourcing it all again." 🦆
*For details of Fran's interior design business and to view her online shop, visit coachhousehome.co.uk.*

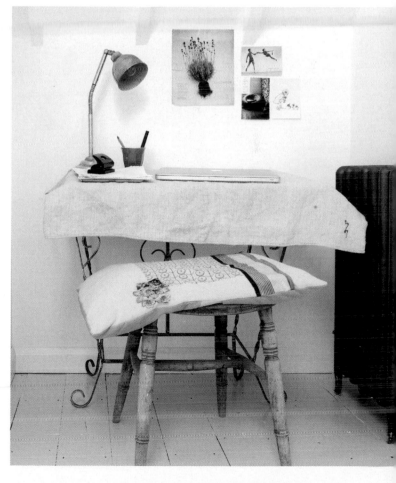

# PROJECTS
## to create

*From sewing a simple curtain to making rustic shelves, you don't need to be an expert to produce your own accessories or repurpose pieces of furniture. Follow these step-by-step projects and have fun creating your own handmade pieces*

# Revamp a hallway

Bring new life to an old console table and place it under a couple of pretty pinboards, styled in a complementing colour

*This old half-moon console table was the perfect size for a small hallway, but years of misuse had left it scratched and battered, and its dark varnish made it feel dated. A coat of satin-finish paint has given it a new look, as well as making it resistant to the knocks and bumps of hallway traffic.*

**YOU WILL NEED**
**old table**
**sandpaper**
**white spirit**
**satin-finish paint**

**1** Sand the table with a medium-grade sandpaper to give the surface a key.
**2** Moisten a soft cloth or kitchen roll with white spirit and wipe down to remove any dirt and dust; allow to dry.
**3** Paint on two coats of hardwearing satin-finish paint (referring to the manufacturer's instructions). Leave to dry.

*A pair of inexpensive cork pinboards covered in a co-ordinating fresh fabric makes a pretty background against which to display arrangements of cards, pictures and quirky memorabilia.*

**YOU WILL NEED**
**cork pinboards**
**satin-finish paint**
**fabric**
**flat-head screwdriver**

**1** Apply two coats of hardwearing satin-finish paint, in the colour of your choice, to the frame of the board.
**2** Cut fabric to cover the board, allowing 1.5cm extra on all sides. Lay it on top and, with a flat-head screwdriver, gently coax the fabric under the frame so it fits snugly.
**3** Attach the ends on the back with pins if required. Hang the boards on the wall.

STYLING BY **CAROLINE REEVES** ASSISTED BY **CELIA STUART-MENTETH** PHOTOGRAPHS BY **SIMON BEVAN**

ROBERT TAVENER

# Paint a floor covering

Add interesting detail to plain flooring with a distinctive rug you have designed yourself

*Draw your pattern free-hand onto a piece of canvas or, if stuck for inspiration, try a ready-made stencil (which can be enlarged to the size you require), then use emulsion paint to colour in the design.*

**YOU WILL NEED**
**plywood**
**piece of cotton duck canvas**
**staple gun or tape**
**emulsion paint**
**stencil**
**acrylic matt varnish**
**carpet mesh**

**1** Cut a piece of 1cm-thick plywood to the size you wish your rug to be. Centre the wood on a piece of primed no 10 cotton duck canvas, allowing 7cm-10cm extra on all sides (the board keeps the canvas taut during painting and drying).
**2** Make sure the primed side of the canvas is face down, away from the wood.
**3** Fold the canvas around the plywood and staple or tape into place, starting from the middle of each side.
**4** Turn the board over and paint the primed canvas surface with a base colour. If you want to give your rug more depth, stipple the paint onto the canvas. When dry, stencil or paint onto the primed and painted surface. Follow with two coats of acrylic matt varnish to seal the canvas.
**5** Remove the canvas from the board, fold the excess underneath and fix in place with double-sided or carpet tape.
**6** Leave to dry for four days before laying on a non-slip carpet pad or mesh. The rug can be cleaned with a damp cloth and mild detergent.

STYLING BY **CAROLINE REEVES** ASSISTED BY **BEN KENDRICK** PHOTOGRAPH BY **LISA COHEN**

STYLING BY **CAROLINE REEVES** ASSISTED BY **CELIA STUART-MENTETH**
PHOTOGRAPH BY **SIMON BEVAN**

# Create a simple headboard

Hang a shabby door sideways to make an inexpensive but stylish board for your bed

*Use a length of dado rail and cheery paint combinations to turn an old door into a bedroom feature. Re-covered with a co-ordinating fabric, a kitchen chair doubles as a useful side table.*

**YOU WILL NEED**
**old door, handles removed**
**eggshell paint**
**paintbrush**
**white spirit**
**dado rail**
**wood glue**
**panel pins**

**1** Cut a door (with equal-sized panels) to the size of your bed. We removed two smaller panels from the door below, so it measured just a little wider than a double bed. If the surface is already painted, sanding it will give a key to which the paint can adhere.
**2** Wipe down with a soft cloth or kitchen roll moistened with white spirit to remove residual dust from the woodwork.
**3** Attach a length of dado rail to the top of the door using wood glue and panel pins, and mitre in two small sections at both ends.
**4** Paint with two coats of eggshell and highlight the panelled sections with toning colours.
**5** Secure the bedhead to the wall with mirror plates and place a baton below, screwed to the wall, to support it.

# Refurbish an old sofa

Give a favourite but tired piece of furniture a facelift with new fabric

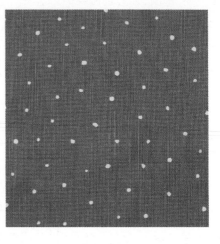

The dark stained woodwork of the sofa pictured opposite has been sanded and polished and its tired cushion covers replaced. An assortment of old frames, painted in tonal shades of blue, creates a unique display behind it.

**YOU WILL NEED**
**sandpaper**
**white spirit**
**beeswax polish**
**fabric, to cover base and cushions**
**staple gun**

**1** Remove the varnish from the woodwork, rubbing medium-grade sandpaper in the direction of the grain. Take care to avoid any canework on the side.
**2** Sand down again with a fine-grade paper until you have a smooth finish.
**3** Vacuum away dust, then moisten a soft cloth or kitchen roll with white spirit and wipe over to remove any residue. Allow to dry. With a soft cloth, buff the frame with a beeswax polish in a circular motion.
**4** Use a staple gun to attach fabric to the base and then re-cover the seat and back cushions with loose covers.

There's no need to buy a staple gun – you can hire one from most DIY companies

STYLING BY **CAROLINE REEVES** ASSISTED BY **CELIA STUART-MENTETH** PHOTOGRAPHS BY **SIMON BEVAN**

# Build rustic kitchen shelves

## Store crockery, glasses and other accessories on simple, repurposed shelving

STYLING BY **CAROLINE REEVES** ASSISTED BY **CELIA STUART-MENTETH** PHOTOGRAPHS BY **SIMON BEVAN**

*Look out for pieces of outdoor fixtures and fittings that can work really well with a country look. In this case, old scaffold planks have been turned into simple shelving. Measure the length you need for a particular corner or wall – you can always cut them to fit. We found the brackets pictured here encrusted with layers of paint and dirt in a salvage yard, and stripped them back to reveal their elegant shapes. Finish the wooden planks with a hardwax oil, which creates a beautiful, easy-to-clean surface.*

**YOU WILL NEED**
**planks of wood**
**sandpaper**
**white spirit**
**hardwax oil**
**old brackets**
**paint stripper**
**metal primer**
**oil eggshell paint**
**rawlplugs**
**screws**

**1** Remove any old nails from the planks.
**2** Prepare the wood with a rough-grade sandpaper and finish with a finer one (or use an electric sander).
**3** Wipe with a soft cloth or kitchen roll moistened with white spirit to remove any residue and allow to dry.
**4** Following the manufacturer's instructions on the tin, apply two coats of Osmo hardwax oil. We used a transparent white, which allows you to see the grain of the wood.
**5** Once dry, buff the wood lightly with fine sandpaper to finish.
**6** For the brackets, use a paint stripper to remove the layers of old colour.
**7** Apply a metal primer and finish with two coats of oil eggshell.
**8** Attach the brackets to the wall using rawlplugs and screws. Sit the wooden planks on top, attaching to the wall as well if necessary.

# Sew a cushion cover

Give old blankets a new lease of life with these easy-to-make home accessories

*Combining two or three colours is particularly effective. The satin trim not only looks lovely but means that there is no need to hem the edges.*

**YOU WILL NEED**
paper
rectangular cushion pad
tape measure or ruler
fabric and paper scissors
blankets, one to dye or two or three
  different-coloured ones
sewing machine and thread
tailor's chalk
pins

**1** Cut a pattern out of paper the same dimensions as your cushion pad, adding 1.5cm for a seam allowance.
**2** For the one-colour side of the cushion cover, chalk around the pattern on your fabric, then cut this shape out.
**3** To create the two-panel side, fold the paper pattern over one-third of the way in. Chalk around this square shape on two different coloured materials, making sure at least one of these is from the edge of the blanket with the satin or stitched trim.
**4** Lay out the main panel, right side up, on a flat surface. Position the two other

pieces on top, ensuring that the best sides of the wool are facing inwards and the raw edges are lined up around the outsides – the satin or stitched trims should be in the middle, as these will form the hemmed opening for your envelope cushion cover. Pin in place and sew all the way round using running stitch, leaving a 1.5cm seam allowance and removing the pins as you go.
**5** Snip across the corners to remove some of the bulk of the fabric, then turn the cover the right way out, iron flat on a suitably low heat and stuff with the cushion pad.

THE FOLLOWING 12 PROJECTS ARE BY **SARAH MOORE**
PHOTOGRAPHS BY **ALUN CALLENDER** STYLING BY **BEN KENDRICK**

# Transform an old case

Pairing everyday objects together can result in an individual piece of furniture

*Here we've used a 1950s picnic case and the legs from an old table: you can also buy these from hydewood.com (and ready-to-top stools for a simpler make). Experiment with the style of legs, and top with hampers, trunks, blanket boxes or crates to get the look you want.*

## YOU WILL NEED

**four legs, reclaimed or new**
**paper, pencil, scissors, craft knife**
**box with smooth solid base**
**tape measure or ruler**
**bradawl**
**flat-headed screws and screwdriver**
**wood glue, PVA glue and brush**
**lining paper**

**1** The legs are attached by screws that are fixed downwards from inside the box. Draw around the top of each leg onto paper and cut out. Use this template to mark out on the bottom of the box, and inside, where the final leg position will be. Make sure these points match up using a tape measure.
**2** Form a slight hole with a bradawl where the screws will go, then begin to screw them into the base of the box, stopping when they are just flush with the bottom surface.
**3** Next, smear a little wood glue onto the top of each leg. One at a time, hold them in place against the box, then screw down to attach firmly. The screws should sit flush with the bottom of the box and the end result should feel stable and rigid. For larger tables, you may want to glue a length of wood between the top of the legs to provide extra support.
**4** Wipe away excess glue, then measure the dimensions of the interior of the box for the lining. Mark these on your paper and cut out. Brush the inside of the box with a thin layer of PVA glue, then position the paper. Trim the top edges neatly with a craft knife.
**5** Make use of any existing fittings in your box for added storage – here, plate and cutlery straps are used to hold fabric and scissors for a novel sewing companion.

# Update a shabby lampbase

An easy but effective method of giving an old table or floor lamp a new style

*You can glue cloth to wood, china or even metal bases. The stand pictured features 3cm-4cm squares of new materials and small offcuts. As a general rule, the more intricate or shaped an area you are trying to cover, the smaller the pieces of fabric need to be. You can apply one style to the whole lamp or strips and squares cut from favourite finds. Alternatively, choose pieces of fabric to match your curtains or bed linen.*

**YOU WILL NEED**
**lamp base**
**fabric in varying patterns**
   **and sizes**
**PVA glue**
**pasting brush**

**1** Working from the top down, brush the part of the stand you are working on with a generous layer of PVA glue, then attach the pieces of material, overlapping them so no surface is visible and using your pasting brush to smooth and stick down the corners. Don't worry if the glue soaks through the fabric, as it becomes invisible when dry.

**2** Leave the lampbase to dry for at least five hours.

**3** You can then add a plain or patterned shade, or create one yourself by covering a new or old frame with fabric (see right). Lengths of ribbon, braids and trimming wound round work well, too.

# Make a simple lampshade

Freshen up a standard lamp by giving a larger shade a different look with natural fabrics

*Make sure there is plenty of room between the material and the bulb to prevent scorching.*

**YOU WILL NEED**
lampshade frame
fabric
tailors' chalk or water-soluble
  sewing pen
scissors, pins, needle, thread
sewing machine
ribbon or cord long enough to go round
  base and top of shade plus few extra cm
strip of fabric ribbon
large safety pin

**1** Measure the height of the frame from the top to the bottom rings, then round the base. Add 15cm to both of these and chalk this oblong onto the wrong side of your chosen fabric. Cut out the shape. Pin then sew the two shorter side edges, right sides together, leaving a 1cm margin. Flatten out the seam edges and press.
**2** Iron a hem of 2cm at the top and bottom of the cylinder. Pin, then sew it in place (this forms the channel for the ribbon or cord).
**3** Turn the cylinder right side out and press.
**4** With scissors, snip through the stitches, 1cm down, into the top and bottom of the cylinder, where the side seams meet, to give access to the drawstring channel.
**5** Cut a length of ribbon or cord to stretch round the shade base and attach a safety pin to the end. Feed this into the channel and push it round until it emerges at the seam. Do the same with the top of the lamp and place the cylinder over the frame.
**6** Pull both ends of the cord together at the base and tighten until the fabric is taut. Tie in a bow and repeat for the top. Move the fabric around till gathered, then secure with a double knot on each cord and trim off the excess. Tuck the ends into the channel and sew up the stitches you snipped earlier.
**7** Tie a ribbon or hemmed length of fabric around the outside of the shade.

# Stitch a hanging tidy

Use this hanging storage for winter accessories to free up valuable peg space for jackets

*Put this near an entrance, attach it to the back of a door or make one in linen for a bathroom or bedroom.*

**YOU WILL NEED**
fabric: 90cm x 40cm for the back
   50cm x 36cm for the pouch
   35cm x 7cm for the band
tape measure, pins, scissors, iron
tailors' chalk or water-soluble
  sewing pen
sewing machine, thread
two 10cm-long ribbons to make the ties

**1** Turn over a 1cm hem around each piece of fabric. Iron flat, then pin. Reduce corner bulk by snipping off just over 1cm from each point. Sew the hems.
**2** Take the pouch fabric and line up one short side on the right-hand side at the bottom of the backing fabric so the two right sides face up. Pin in place and stitch the right-hand seam, removing the pins. Over-sew several times at the top (seams need to be strong here).
**3** Repeat the process on the left side. The fabric should not sit tightly across.
**4** Flatten the pouch evenly (fabric will hang over the side seams). Iron, then pinch the extra material inwards, creating a V-shape or concertina effect. Pin it down on each side and sew along the bottom, through the folded side seams, to create a pouch.
**5** Hand- or machine-stitch through the folded V-shape seam at the sides, just at the top, to prevent it falling open when filled.
**6** To create the flap, lift and fold the backing fabric towards you, about 15cm above the opening of the pouch, so the reverse sides of this section meet. Press, pin and sew down each side of the flap, then across the width of the backing fabric, to close the flap.
**7** To attach the band, measure 15cm from the top seam down and 2.5cm in from each side. Pin the hemmed strip at each end and in the middle. Stitch across at these points.
**8** Sew ribbon loops to the top for hanging.

# Construct underbed storage

Make the most of the space beneath beds with these drawers, fashioned from old furniture

*Remember to include the casters when measuring the height of a drawer to check it will fit the space available.*

**YOU WILL NEED**
**paint, paintbrush**
**sandpaper**
**clear wax**
**chalk paint in grey and white**
**soft cloth**
**drawer, casters**
**pencil, bradawl**
**screws, screwdriver**
**tape measure or ruler**
**wallpaper or old map for lining**
**scissors, craft knife**
**PVA glue and brush**

**1** Chalk paint is a water-based and low-odour option for furniture and is very easy to use. For a vintage look, there's no need to prime or sand a surface – just remove any dirt or loose material before you start. The drawer here has been painted, sanded and sealed with clear wax, then rubbed with a little white chalk paint, using a soft cloth, to create the worn look; the top edges have been painted, then left, for a clean finish. Try Annie Sloan for paints and waxes, and more tips on how to achieve a similar look (anniesloan.com).
**2** Place your drawer upside down with the casters in their finished positions. Make a pencil mark where each screw

will go, then repeat using a bradawl to form a slight hole.
**3** Screw the casters on firmly at all four points.
**4** Turn the drawer the right way up. Measure the interior dimensions for the lining, mark them onto the back of a length of wallpaper or an old map, then cut out the panels.
**5** Brush the drawer's interior with a thin layer of PVA glue. Position your paper pieces and gently smooth out bumps. Trim off any excess with a craft knife for a smart finish.
**6** Once dry, fill with blankets, bedding or toys and store under your bed until needed.

# Make a jewellery frame

Store your favourite items in one place with this decorative display – a work of art in itself

*This jewellery frame has pockets folded into the material that provide a pretty way to store – and display – each item. You can use vintage floral fabric but any patterned material will work, as long as it's not too thick.*

**YOU WILL NEED**
frame with a solid back that can either
   stand or be hung
fabric just over twice the length of,
   and 10cm wider than, your frame
ruler, scissors and pins
iron
sewing machine
double-sided sticky tape or fabric glue
needle and thread

1 Cut your fabric to size, then turn over a narrow hem on all sides. Iron flat, pin in place and sew, removing the pins as you go.
2 For the pockets, lay the material out, right side facing up. Pleat, leaving sufficient distance between the top edge and the first pouch so it will fit inside your frame, and bearing in mind the size of the items you want to store – you could make some pouches deeper than others to hold bigger things. Use your ruler as a guide.
3 Iron the pockets flat and pin in place at the sides. Using running stitch, sew down each edge of the fabric to secure the folds, then go from top to bottom at

intervals across your material, to form individual pouches. Remove the pins as you go and press again.
4 To display in your frame, attach a few strips of double-sided sticky tape to the solid back panel, peel off the backing paper, then place onto the wrong side of your fabric. Smooth the cloth down, ensuring it is secured. Reposition until you are happy.
5 Fold the overhanging edges of material over the back of the frame, top and bottom first, then the sides, and hand-sew the corners together to create a neat finish.
6 Put the pocket panel into the frame and fix the back in place with the clips.

# Craft a mosaic heart

## Reclaim a little pleasure from broken fragments of crockery with these pretty coasters

*There's no need to feel disheartened when crockery is broken. Keep hold of the pieces and use them to make handy drinks coasters.*

### YOU WILL NEED

**goggles or protective glasses
and gloves**
**broken china**
**tile cutters**
**wooden heart or other shape
(available from shops such
as Hobbycraft)**
**paper, pencil**
**small mixing bowls**
**tile cement, stirrers and grout**
**palette knife and disposable cloth**

**1** Wear goggles and gloves to protect your eyes and hands. Start by snipping square or triangular shapes from your china with the tile cutters, looking for particular designs and pretty details – using just the edge of the blades produces the best pieces.
**2** Draw around the wooden heart on paper, then arrange the fragments on this, building up a 'crazy paving' pattern and leaving small gaps in between each tile. Choose pieces from the edge of the ceramics for the borders to give a cleaner finish. Play around with the design until you are happy with it.
**3** Put your gloves on and, in a small bowl, mix the cement according to the instructions, stirring in water until it is smooth. Spread a layer 2mm-3mm deep over the wooden heart, depending on the thickness of your china.
**4** Transfer the arrangement of china pieces from your paper pattern to the heart, then push them into the cement, so the surfaces are level. Leave to dry for at least two hours. In the meantime, scrape and wipe out the bowl before washing it, putting the leftover cement in a bin (do not pour down the sink).
**5** Again wearing gloves, mix up the grout. Smooth this in between the china pieces, applying more than you need. With a palette knife, remove any excess, then wipe the tiles clean. Once dry, buff to get rid of any marks. As with the cement, do not pour any remaining grout down your sink.

# Design your own artwork

Use fragments of favourite motifs to form striking framed displays for the wall

*Cut shapes from wallpaper, music scores or old maps, drawing designs on the reverse before snipping, and use plain or pretty paper for the background.*

**YOU WILL NEED**
**card or wallpaper**
**scissors, pencil**
**paper shapes**
**double-sided pads**
**box frame, with or without glass**

**1** Cut a piece of thick card or wallpaper to fit inside your frame. Arrange your cut-out paper shapes on top, leaving a sufficient border so your design fits within the frame.
**2** Mark a small cross on the paper under the centre of each shape and place one or two double-sided sticky pads on top. Fold each shape to give it depth, then peel off the backing cover from the sticky pads and position your shapes on top.
**3** Put your artwork inside the frame and secure the back with the clips provided, so it is ready to hang.

# Update cupboard linings

Transform old cupboards and wardrobes with pieces of vintage wallpaper and strips of fabric

*For darker and unpainted woods, lining with paper will create a lighter effect. You can update the edges of shelves in a similar way, attaching strips of fabric, wallpaper, gift wrap, postcards or maps.*

**YOU WILL NEED**
**ruler**
**fabric or paper**
**pencil**
**scissors or craft knife**
**paintbrush or kitchen sponge**
**PVA glue**
**drawing pins**

**1** To line your cupboard or drawer, measure the area you would like to cover, then mark these dimensions onto your fabric or paper, and cut out. Alternatively, you could use lots of smaller patterned pieces to create a collage effect.
**2** Make sure the surface to be decorated is clean and dust-free, then, using a paintbrush or kitchen sponge, apply a thin layer of glue to it. Position your paper and, working from the centre out, smooth any creases or air bubbles gently towards the edges. To seal, coat it with another thin layer of glue and leave to dry. If using

smaller pieces, stick them down one at a time, then seal the surface when the whole area has been covered.
**3** Once dry, use a craft knife or scissors to trim any excess pieces of paper from the edges. Repeat the entire process on all of the other panels you wish to decorate.
**4** For shelf edges, measure the length of the shelf and cut an appropriately sized strip of fabric or paper, making a feature of any pattern by cutting around it to create a scalloped effect. Attach with glue, using drawing pins to keep it in place until dry.

# Sew pretty drawstring bags

Made from scraps of fabric, these are perfect for storing essential kitchen ingredients

*Why hide staple ingredients away when, with a bit of fabric and ribbon, you can turn them into items worthy of display? Use these bags to store spices, sugar or flour in their packaging or poured in, with a label in the pocket.*

**YOU WILL NEED**
strong cotton, ticking or twill fabric, plus small scraps for the pockets
ruler, scissors, pinking shears
sewing machine and thread
iron, pins
ribbon for drawstring
large safety pin
needle and thread

1 Cut your fabric into rectangles, using a ruler to ensure each bag is made out of pieces that are the same size. Use different materials for the back and front sections, if you wish. For small pouches, ideal for storing spices, cut shapes 15cm x 12cm in size, while for larger bags, for items such as sugar or flour, 24cm x 20cm dimensions work best.
2 From your scrap fabric, use pinking shears to cut out a suitably sized square to make a pocket. Secure this on three sides to the material that will form the front panel of your bag, making sure the right sides are facing up, then hand- or machine-sew in place. If you don't have pinking shears, hem the edges of the pocket fabric first.

3 Iron and sew a 1cm-1.5cm hem on the top edges of your rectangles, leaving a channel wide enough to thread your ribbon through to create a drawstring.
4 Lay the front and back panels, right sides together, and pin the sides and bottom edge in place. Sew, removing the pins as you go, starting and stopping just below the hem through which the drawstring will run.
5 Attach a safety pin to one end of the ribbon to thread it through the channel. Tie the ends of the ribbon together, turn the bag the right way out, then press. To neaten up the edges of the drawstring hems, tuck the fabric in and finish with a couple of hand stitches.

# Make a silk scarf curtain

Sew favourite pieces of sheer fabrics together for beautiful window treatments

*Hang these at windows or use to divide rooms, form a canopy over beds or as a simple throw. You can often find silk scarves in charity shops and markets – or choose other fabrics, if you prefer. It's also worth trying specialist online sellers such as Vintage Highlights (stores.ebay.co.uk/vintage-highlights).*

**YOU WILL NEED**
tape measure
scarves of similar sizes
sewing machine
masking tape or pins
iron
net-curtain wire and hook fitting, or strong woven tape, large safety pin and hooks

**1** Measure your window, or the area you want to cover, to work out how many scarves you need. For a gathered finish, add at least half the width again to the measurement.
**2** Arrange your scarves on a large flat surface so they form the desired pattern, overlapping the edges by a couple of centimetres on all sides.
**3** Taking a row at a time, create strips of scarves – which you will then sew together to create one big panel. Use masking tape, or pins if you prefer, to secure the scarves, then straight-stitch down each join, removing the tape or pins as you go.
**4** Repeat with each row, then sew these together in the same way to create a panel. When this is complete, turn over a 2cm hem at the top and stitch in place so you have a channel.
**5** Run a net-curtain wire through this gap, or, alternatively, attach a length of strong tape to a safety pin and feed it through, then hang it up on hooks fixed to the sides of your windowframe.

# Meet the
## MAKERS

Discover an array of designers and artisans producing beautiful crafts for the home: eye-catching ceramics, patterned fabrics, avian artwork, woven baskets, colourful quilts and exquisite hand-blocked wallpapers

# The tale of a
# SHROPSHIRE POTTER

*Uniting her love of food and horticulture,
Rachel Barker's clean, contemporary ceramics
echo the elemental beauty of nature*

WORDS BY **HESTER LACEY** | PHOTOGRAPHS BY **ALUN CALLENDER**

Most people might imagine that a potter's kitchen would feature an immaculate range of their work, but Rachel Barker's cupboards are filled with prototypes. Each understated design complements the others, and draws inspiration from the nature outside her door: the cranesbill scrambling over the garden of her red-brick cottage in the grounds of Shropshire estate Walcot Hall, the coriander growing in her herb bed, or the rosy blush of a crab apple. Some influences are more subtle – the mark of a saw in wood, or a raindrop's rivulet path down a window pane, but all are translated into elegant pieces refreshingly free of any trace of chintz or kitsch.

Rachel's pieces are not just about looking good on the table, however; they have to feel nice in the hand, and this is why she tests each new design at home. "There's no point simply looking at the shape of a mug – you have to feel it. My designs are about enjoyment. I'm throwing and making all the time, and some things work, some don't," she says. As well as beautiful to look at and satisfying to hold, Rachel's ceramics are supremely practical and meant to be used. While she doesn't cater to the more formal end of the market ("I will never make a soup tureen or a dish for a gravy boat!"), her clean, contemporary shapes and fresh colours include everything for daily use: plates, jugs, storage jars, bowls and mugs, plus endearingly chunky, rounded butter boxes and 'herb bricks' – stylish containers for your windowsill crop of basil, mint or parsley.

Each morning, Rachel walks from her cottage across a sheep-grazed meadow to a little workshop hidden behind a green-painted wooden door that leads to the estate's walled garden. Inside, shelves of freshly fired mugs and bowls sit alongside jugs of pencils and brushes, and jars of paint and slip (liquid clay). The woodburning stove that once kept the estate's gardeners' fingers from freezing still stands in one corner. Rachel's designs start life as a sketch taped to the wall above her wheel, and each creation is hands-on from start to finish.

Unusually, Rachel decorates her thrown pieces before they go into the kiln, using a technique called sgraffito (the Italian for 'scratched'). "For textures and colours, I find there is a much softer, more responsive quality when I decorate on raw clay," she explains. She allows it to dry until the surface resembles leather, and then etches directly into it, freehand. "I use a pointed tool to scratch the pattern, then flood it with colour. Next, I scratch back the surface with a penknife to reveal the coloured design; it's a method that gives a lovely quality of line and texture. I still find it exciting seeing the finished pieces come out of the kiln."

Before Rachel and her partner Andrew – who takes care of the business side of the enterprise – moved to Shropshire in 2004, they lived in Bristol. Despite enjoying the city, Rachel hankered after greener spaces. "I needed more room, more air, and I wanted to be fed visually by the landscape," she explains. Now, all the grounds of Walcot Hall lie outside her front door and she can wander the network of paths through the estate's woods and meadows at will. "The move has been incredibly fruitful," she says. "It's down to little details, like sitting in the garden looking at the fine markings on an onion stalk. I don't represent the wider landscape in a formal way, but I definitely use elements from it."

Everything Rachel makes in her workshop is, of course, a one-off; but, even with three kilns, she ▷

can't personally produce her entire range. Plus, as she notes, "you can't hand-make every single piece unless the prices are exorbitant – and why shouldn't good design be affordable and accessible?" She decided to enlist a long-established company in Stoke-on-Trent, the traditional heartland of British pottery, to make her creamware, a high-quality English earthenware. The skills of the Stoke potters, she says, are crucial to the handmade nature of her ceramics, even though English production is expensive in comparison with using companies in, for example, the Far East. "Each piece is slip-cast by hand; a man with a very big pot of liquid clay pours it out," Rachel explains. "Although it's an industrial process, it's done in the traditional way. Stoke's pottery culture goes back hundreds of years and the work is of such a high standard." She similarly uses a small Midlands firm to make up her textile range, which includes aprons, oven gloves and tea cosies.

Rachel studied fine art at degree level, and specialised in printmaking. It has, she says, proved surprisingly useful not to have studied ceramics formally. "I wasn't taught what I should and shouldn't do, so I was prepared to take risks. What I bring to the craft is my own instinct. It ties the factory in knots!" she laughs. "They tell me I can't do this or that – but then they manage it somehow." After she left college, Rachel lived in Italy for several years, settling in Milan, Rome and Tuscany, and was introduced to traditional Italian pottery. "When I came back, I wanted to make a living through being creative, and ceramics seemed the obvious choice. Everybody needs a plate, and it's such an enjoyable medium." Pottery also seemed to tie together perfectly Rachel's twin passions for food and horticulture. "While I was in Italy, I tended English people's gardens when they were away." This experience helped to kindle Rachel's love of gardening, and she later went on to pass the RHS General Certificate in Horticulture in 2002. However, her time there also taught her important lessons about our relationship with food. "There is a great emphasis on sitting together and eating with family and friends in Italy, and although my ceramics are very English, this is a significant thread in my work. The other great emphasis was on eating what grows around you at the right time of year – an idea we are finally getting to grips with now, but it was quite an education 20 years ago!"

Back in Shropshire, Rachel's own plot is a riot of flowers, all beautifully fitting together in terms of shape and colour, but behind the high green gates of the walled garden, she grows a range of produce to keep her kitchen supplied from spring to autumn with squashes, courgettes, leeks, tomatoes and fennel. "Designing ceramics for food, cultivating vegetables and eating them are all closely connected," Rachel says. "It's about simple pleasures that help enhance daily life." 🦆
*Rachel Barker (01588 680555; rachelbarker.com).*

OPPOSITE Rachel gleans inspiration from her surroundings. THIS PAGE Designs start life as pencil sketches pinned to the wall

# The power of PRINT

With a dedication to design, Fiona Howard uses traditional skills such as monoprint and cut-paper techniques to create her vibrant homeware collections

WORDS BY **CELIA STUART-MENTETH**
PHOTOGRAPHS BY **NICK CARTER**
STYLING BY **HESTER PAGE**

MOUNTAIN
FLOWERS

MOUNTAIN
FLOWERS

THIS PAGE AND OPPOSITE
Fiona creates her
intricate designs for use
on upholstery, including
Dandelion Clocks
(above), and cushions,
such as Spring
Angelica (centre)

Looking at Fiona Howard's contemporary, colourful prints, you wouldn't think she had very much in common with the 19th-century textile artist William Morris and his traditional motifs inspired by nature. Ranging from bone-china mugs and birchwood trays to bags and tea towels, her fabrics and accessories in blues and fuchsias, yellows and greens seem a world apart from the muted Arts & Crafts palette of Morris. However, his extraordinary skill in weaving together plant shapes to create harmonious, repeating patterns is just what textile designer Fiona achieves with her vibrant linocuts based on stylised flowers and foliage.

"I am always looking at the plant forms around me and love to gather flowers, leaves, seed pods and seaweed," she explains. Fiona draws inspiration from a variety of sources, including beds and borders in friends' gardens as well as vintage botanical illustrations and pebbles brought back from surfing trips to Cornwall. Her sketchbooks are brimming with a seemingly eclectic collection of ideas: honeysuckle seen in a British hedgerow, perhaps, or an unusual-looking seed pod found on a walk. This passion for nature is captured in her intricate, eye-catching designs, including Spring Angelica, Wild Pods, Hydrangea and Waterlily.

Fiona lives and works in an elegant Regency terraced house in Brighton, with her husband Simon and children Eddie and Olly. The sitting room doubles as her studio and is filled with natural light, while the neutral walls act as a backdrop for her work. The pinboard above her desk is full of ideas to tap into, from floral postcards and paint charts to bold designs and swatches of fabric.

The physical process involved in creating her prints is an important aspect of her work. "I use my hands in everything I do," she says, "whether it's colouring my own papers or hand-cutting a lino." Each design can take more than a week to produce, starting with preparatory sketches that she re-works until the shapes flow as a repeating pattern. Once this is achieved, a mirror image is traced onto a piece of lino, which Fiona carefully cuts using a chisel and gouge. When inked, the lino is printed onto previously coloured paper sample sheets and left to dry on her studio floor for 24 hours. This traditional technique is extremely important to Fiona. "There is so much that's computer generated in our world today and I think true crafts are once again being appreciated for their skill," she says. When clients look through her portfolio, they often like to smooth their hand over a design and "feel the sense of craftsmanship".

Fiona has enjoyed considerable success during her 25 years as a freelance textile designer, working with companies such as John Lewis, Colefax and Fowler, Marks & Spencer, Harlequin and Pierre Frey. Her retro Dandelion Clocks print for Sanderson has become one of the most well known, and appears on curtains, furniture, bedlinen and even biscuit tins. Although her designs are clever and often intricate, they also have a light, upbeat quality. Each one is a beautiful way to bring the outside in and add new colour and life to a room. ◢

*To find out more about Fiona's work, call 01273 731646 or visit fionahoward. com. Prices start at £35/m for fabric or £10 for a mug or tea towel.*

# A bird's eye view

Gloucestershire woodcarver Michael Lythgoe draws on his passion for ornithology
and traditional craftsmanship to create a world of avian artistry

WORDS BY **LOUISE ELLIOTT**  |  PHOTOGRAPHS BY **ANDREW MONTGOMERY**

Michael Lythgoe can't resist a bird in flight. Even when he's hard at work in his Gloucestershire workshop sculpting his smooth, sinuous pieces, he regularly grabs a pair of binoculars to track the flocks of birds passing overhead on their way to the Severn Estuary, a few miles away. "I love their aerodynamic quality, the way you can identify different species by their flight patterns," he says. And it is this sense of movement that he seeks to capture in his carved wooden birds. "I'm not trying to duplicate nature, more to suggest the impression of catching a glimpse of a bird in flight." Native British birds are his subject matter, particularly those with graceful, curved forms and long, elegant beaks, necks and tails – gannets with their distinctive dagger bills, inky black and pure white avocets, curlews with their smoothly curved beaks, common sandpipers, lonely-looking herons, diminutive dippers and long-legged avocets with their upturned bills are all among his avian repertoire.

There are single birds perched on tall posts but also flocks of the same species, each one in a slightly different flight position to create movement and interest. Michael carves from reclaimed timber to increase the sense of texture and often mounts his birds on striking pieces of driftwood, which he spends hours hunting for on the banks of the River Severn. "The high spring tides wash up a lot but you have to search hard for the good bits," he explains. "I keep my eyes peeled for interesting shapes, parts of trees with unusual root and branch formations, those that have been bleached by the sun and convey the essence of the shore. I couldn't carve with the driftwood, though, as it can lack stability."

A trained engineer, Michael's interest in ornithology began in the early 1970s when, just married, he moved from the Wirral to Shropshire with his wife, Carol-Anne, and started exploring the countryside on foot. "I took up photography as a hobby to record the forests and woodland we were discovering but soon began to concentrate on birds," he says.

This fascination with nature developed even further when the couple moved to St Catharines near Lake Ontario in Canada, where Michael had been offered an engineering post in a shipyard. "It was on the shores of the lake and migrating wildfowl would pass over in great flocks," he remembers. A trip to Cape Cod took his pastime in a new direction when he unearthed some early 20th-century decoy birds in a ▷

OPPOSITE Michael in his studio putting the finishing touches to one of his graceful cranes. THIS PAGE Curved lines characterise his work

more detailed carvings in favour of the simpler, more stylised, smooth-bodied pieces he had begun producing: "The replicas could never be accurate enough for me and I wanted to create more artistically inspired pieces. In this craft, less is definitely more."

Today, the eye of the ornithologist, the engineer and the artist are all evident in his graceful pieces, each one sharing a sense of natural beauty and simplicity. Every bird demands hours of craftsmanship using mostly basic tools. Inside his workshop, converted from the family garage, Michael echoes the tradition of the early carvers – everything is close to hand. Alongside pieces of family memorabilia, there is just room for an old, heavily scored wooden bench strewn with chisels, files, drills, knives, pieces of sandpaper and an iron vice.

To keep up with demand, Michael now spends so many hours of the day carving that he doesn't have as much time to spend bird-watching as he once did. "When we first moved here, I was always down at the Severn Estuary watching the wildfowl and the waders. Fortunately, there's a world of inspiration in the skies above our garden." ❧
*Michael Lythgoe (01452 712080; michaellythgoe.com).*

THIS PAGE Michael spends hours shaping and sanding each piece by hand; an old decoy duck OPPOSITE A striking egret

junk shop, drawn by their primitive, rough-hewn quality.

Decoy carving began in North America in the early 19th century as a way of luring wildfowl. "Even today, many towns on the Eastern Seaboard of the US and Canada have a decoy carving club, so I set out to find out as much as I could about the craft and its history," Michael says. Gradually, he began whittling his own carvings to send back to his family in England as Christmas presents, never dreaming that his new-found hobby would develop into a full-time business.

In 1986, Michael and Carol-Anne returned to England with their young family (daughter Sara, then two-and-a-half, and son Michael, one). "I thought more and more about becoming a craftsman." At this stage he was mainly producing extremely detailed pieces with intricately carved feathers, painted in authentic colours. Each one took up to four weeks to make but he slowly built up enough stock to sell at craft shows and agricultural fairs, where he also began to take commissions.

A turning point came when he was offered a shared exhibition with wildlife artist Jonathan Sainsbury at the William Marler Gallery in Cirencester in 1989. It was a sell-out. At this point he decided to abandon his

"I'm not trying to duplicate nature,
more to suggest the impression
of catching a glimpse of one of these
beautiful birds in flight"

# Folk art on the farm

Jo Colwill has pieced together a thriving diversification scheme to bolster income from her dairy herd – craft classes that celebrate the skill of quiltmaking with the chance to create a handmade heirloom of your own

WORDS BY **CAROLINE REES** | PHOTOGRAPHS BY **ALUN CALLENDER**

LEFT Many of Jo's quilting designs are inspired by rural life and the countryside surrounding her Cornish farmhouse. OPPOSITE The farm's dairy herd often features in Jo's work

inspirational countryside. From the gazebo in the vegetable garden, there is a picture-postcard view of Launceston, with its castle outlined on the horizon. The lofty timber-framed workroom is home to quilts, fabrics, pattern books and sewing paraphernalia, while the shop is a stitcher's paradise of buttons, trimmings and patchwork pieces. The café is a tranquil communal meeting place, serving produce from the farm.

Although there is a long folk-art tradition of quilt-making around the world, it is often associated with groups of Victorian women salvaging scraps of material to make do and mend. But Jo has noticed a resurgence of interest in the past few years. "People come to escape from the day-to-day problems of life," she says, "but possibly they are also looking for a more productive use of their free time than just sitting on a beach or whatever. Something made personally means so much more than anything you can buy, and recycling is an important element of it now."

With all the time involved in crafting a quilt, the finished article often becomes a personal statement. In Jo's big farm design, for example, the cartoonish quality draws you in, though her worries about the future of the countryside are illustrated with a huge question mark and a tumble of menacing colours that represent weeds. "You put your life and soul into it," Jo says. "People speak through their quilts in a way."

Jo, who grew up locally, had two loves as a child: horses and sewing. "I practically lived at the riding stables," she says. "But I also loved fabric and made my own dolls' clothes." She went on to teach riding – she still keeps three horses – but turned her attention to quilt-making when she married and moved into the draughty, 400-year old

One of Jo Colwill's most ambitious picture quilts depicts her and her husband Stephen dreaming of what they would miss about their rural lifestyle if they were forced to give up farming. Amid the landscape of hills, a cow peers over the gate, while a horse and cart passes by and Jo tends her garden. Employing quilting, appliqué and stitching techniques, it is an exquisitely executed example of modern folk art. "Everyday things inspire me," Jo says. "I take my dogs out and when I see cobwebs on the grass or the moon coming through the trees, I can't get home quickly enough to start sewing."

Jo and Stephen are tenants on a 120-acre organic dairy farm near Launceston in Cornwall. While Stephen attends to the livestock, Jo runs Cowslip Workshops, which offers craft classes, attracting textile lovers from both home and abroad. She has been quilting for 30 years but it wasn't until 1996 that Cowslip graduated from occasional gatherings around her antique oak dining-table to a full-time business. "It started off with one class and got busier and busier through word of mouth," Jo recalls.

Like many farmers after the foot-and-mouth crisis of 2001, the couple looked at how to diversify, adding first a shop and then a café. It's an exciting enterprise to find down a farm track. There's a maze of rustic outbuildings, little passageways and garden 'rooms', all surrounded by

Newhouse Farm, where her husband's family have been tenants since 1907. "It needed a homely touch," Jo explains. "Farmers never want to spend anything on a house – they'll buy a new tractor but not curtains, so I made my own. And then I made my first quilt, just cut-out diamonds of dressmaking fabric stitched over paper. I'm rather horrified at it now."

She persevered and honed her skills by attending classes and meeting other quilters. Her second effort, a sampler quilt, was borrowed for a magazine shoot by the local home-interiors shop and was snapped up by a customer. Instead of selling it, though, Jo swapped it for a bed. She hasn't looked back.

Workshops, taught by her and by guest tutors, range from Basic Appliqué to Stitching an Autumn Landscape. "I love meeting people and you learn as much as you give," Jo says. She doesn't impose pure quilting on beginners: instead of turning every edge under,

she suggests adhesive and a decorative stitch to speed up the process. "There is nothing right or wrong in quilting. My aim is that people go home clutching something they have made in a day."

The bulk of Jo's creations are class samples, which subsequently sell in the shop. "I do little sketches, then a big drawing to create templates," she says. "I just make it up as I go along. I've got a stash of fabric, including recycled clothes. I use a machine to piece the bits together, then do the intricate parts by hand."

Designs that Jo can't bear to part with are displayed around the farmhouse, including a Baltimore block quilt that details her family history. "Some people want to be textile 'artists' but I just do it because I love it," she says. "You can't really make money out of quilts anyway. Because of the time involved, it's hard to charge even £5 an hour. I did a wholecloth quilt for a house round

here, taking designs from their lovely old bed. It took 990 hours."

Although Jo now employs 15 staff, she mucks in with most tasks. As well as stitching and teaching, she stocks the shop and helps out at lambing time. Late at night is when she gets the chance to be alone with her sewing: "I go into the workroom, the dogs settle under the table and I stitch away."

Cowslip's success bolsters the income from the farm, but it has made inroads into family life, so Jo is keen to involve her husband as much as possible. Hosting community events, such as wassailing evenings and apple days, helps to do that. And the location adds interest to outsiders coming for classes: they keep dairy cows, beef cattle and sheep. "People love seeing the animals," Jo says. "The farm and the workshops support each other. One without the other just wouldn't be the same." *Cowslip Workshops (01566 772654; cowslipworkshops.co.uk).*

# Beauty & utility

*On her Denbighshire farm, Ruth Pybus uses skill and strength
to turn coppiced oak into striking woven baskets – each one
a glorious reminder of our rural past*

WORDS BY **DIONA GREGORY** | PHOTOGRAPHS BY **ALUN CALLENDER**

Picture a basketmaker at work and you might imagine a quietly industrious scene: a woman indoors deftly weaving fine strands of willow, a mug of tea close to hand. But Ruth Pybus's method involves considerably more drama and significantly less comfort. On this January morning, the craftswoman is busy in the snow-covered grounds of the 70-acre Denbighshire farm she shares with her partner David, preparing her materials and dealing with fire, timber and axes. A water-filled cattle trough, heated underneath by furious flames, contains trunks of oak that she has split – or cleaved – lengthways into quarters or 'billets', which are simmering until they are soft enough for her to strip. Her

extraordinary efforts are an attempt to help keep alive the ancient art of making swills: sturdy baskets crafted from oak ribbons, a traditional countryside practice. "After felling and chopping the trees, it takes two days to soak and prepare the wood – that's before I even think about weaving," Ruth explains, as she watches the blend of steam and smoke rise and disappear into the bright, bitter day.

Seeing her in action, it's clear that working with wood is her calling. "I get such a thrill from turning a stout tree into thin, malleable strips of wood and weaving these together to create a sturdy basket," she says. Not only are the rustic designs produced using sustainable materials, swills can last many years if looked after. Placed upside down, the

baskets of the past were strong enough for even a hefty man to sit on in the fields while eating his bread and cheese. Swills came into their own on the land when lifting potatoes or broadcasting seed. They were favoured, too, during the industrial revolution for use both in factories and in the docks. On the domestic front, the swill was indispensable, handy for holding logs, as a cradle and for carrying laundry. Amazingly, in expert hands, it was feasible to weave them so that they were watertight; some think the name derives from this association with swilling washing water.

Today, they are often used to gather vegetables or as decorative items around the home. "The finished article, while being ultimately practical, looks simple and beautiful – that's if I've done my job properly," Ruth says. In a pleasing, circular way, her own swills are used to store the hand tools needed to make them. At her oak stool beside the trough, she is cutting a steaming, piping-hot piece of oak into thin strips with the riving knife. Now that the wood has boiled in the trough for a few hours, it is damp enough to cut into pieces an inch in width. "Riving involves prising the wood apart, which tears it along the grain," she explains. It takes deft strokes – and much practice – to produce consistent ribbons of precise slenderness. The slightly thicker ones for the baskets' 'ribs' are called spelks; the thinner pieces are taws. Most of the prepared wood is stored – Ruth processes enough for six baskets at a time. The oak is then soaked once more overnight to make it flexible enough to be woven – "A good thin strip of damp oak is like supple leather" – and tied around a hazel hoop, which she has bent into shape with steam, the curvature of which defines the basket's proportions. "The old boys could turn out half a dozen every day; it takes me two to make just one. But I am getting quicker," she says.

Ruth's dedication to her craft has involved not only learning the ancient artisan skill, but growing, tending and harvesting the mixed broadleaf trees that David planted on his land – hillsides between the coast and the mountains on the edge of Snowdonia – around 20 years ago. "There's sweet chestnut and ash, which are both used for timber as well as the hazel I need for the swills, but good-quality oak is hard to get hold of, so I buy that from basketmaker Owen Jones."

Along with Ruth's swills, the couple also make charcoal, selling it locally and, in addition to farming his land, David designs and manages woodland for other local farmers, while they team up to carry out contract hedge-laying together. Wood really does seem to pervade every aspect of their lives. 🦆
*Ruth Pybus (07909 078730; framebaskets.co.uk).*
*The 22-inch-wide swills cost £55 and the 15-inch-wide shopper-style design costs £50.*

OPPOSITE The farm lies on the edge of Snowdonia. THIS PAGE Ruth uses weaving and cutting techniques put into practice centuries ago to produce decorative and functional baskets

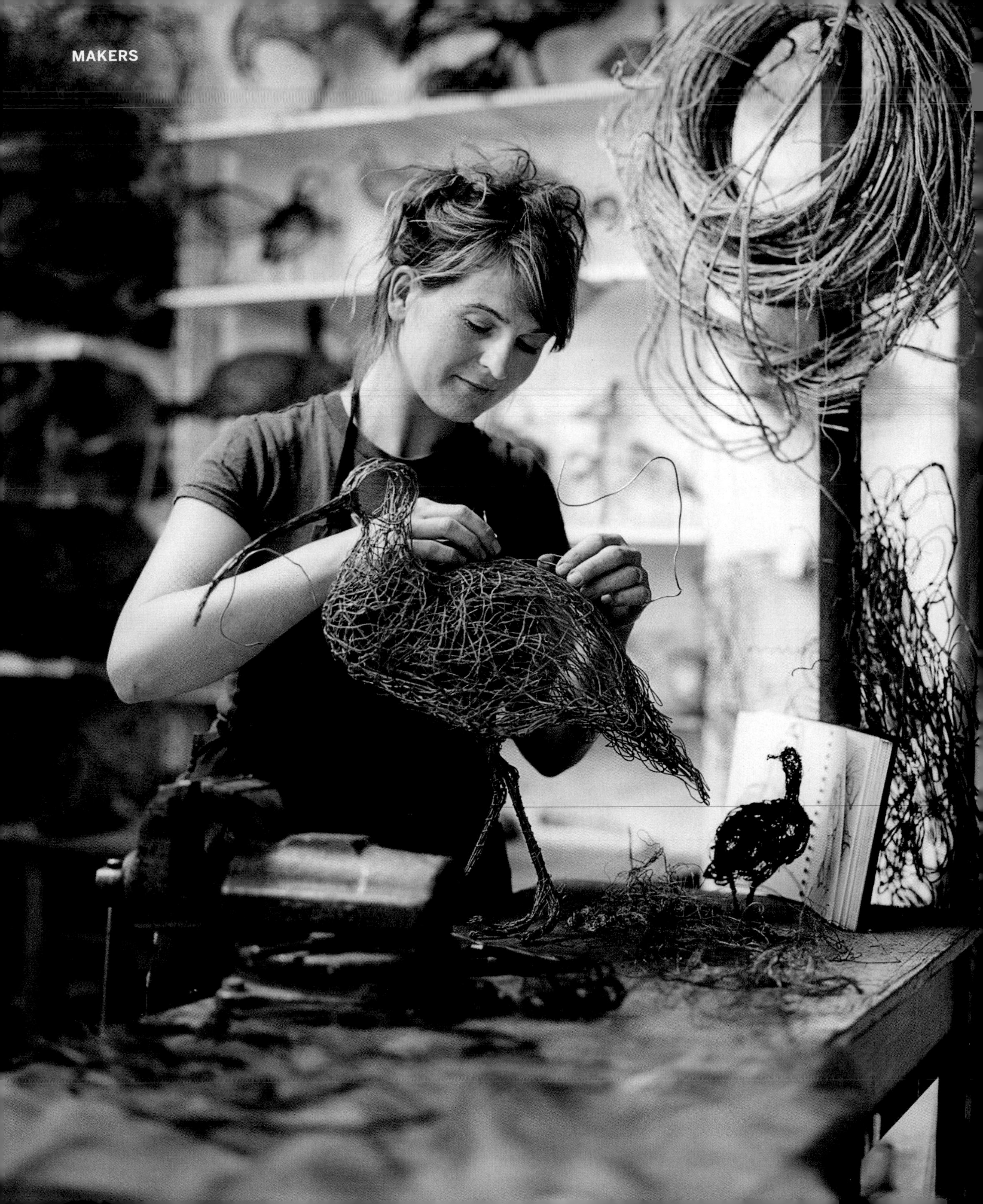

# *Flights*
# OF FANCY

*From curved-billed curlews to*

*flocks of starlings soaring*

*through the sky, Celia Smith*

*creates beautiful artworks for the*

*home from lengths of scrap metal,*

*twisting and shaping the wire to*

*give each bird a sense of*

*movement and character*

WORDS BY **RUTH CHANDLER**
PHOTOGRAPHS BY **ANDREW MONTGOMERY**

## "Observing a bird in its natural environment is the best way to get an idea of its shape"

Surrounded by an arc of barnacle geese lit up with a flash of spring sunlight, Celia Smith opens the leather case at her feet and untangles a mass of wire. Studying the handsome monochrome birds in front of her, she rapidly twists lengths of copper with nothing but a pair of pliers and her hands, capturing their shape in a basic frame, and directing her gaze from one to the other as each changes posture.

At Slimbridge Wildfowl & Wetlands Trust in Gloucestershire, she is in her element. The centre is home to the world's largest collection of swans, ducks and geese, providing the young bird sculptor with an endless source of subject matter. Though Celia occasionally draws with pencil, she usually cuts to the chase and delineates the lines of her subjects with wire. Back at her studio on a farm in Wiltshire, she works up larger pieces, making a basic frame from chicken or fencing wire. "I fiddle with these for hours – it's essential to get them right," she says. She works over the frame using one length of wire, avoiding the need to solder pieces together, wrapping it round the legs to create the right thickness, bending it to make the joints. Through sharp observation, she captures the exact camber of a curlew's beak, spread of a mallard's foot and profile of a swan's head, while each twist glints in the light, suggesting movement, imbuing the sculptures with a sense of every bird's character.

It was the assortment of chickens and a tangle of fencing wire on her parents' dairy and arable farm in Gloucestershire that first inspired Celia to sculpt birds in this material. While living at home, having finished her degree in fine art sculpture at London's Wimbledon School of Art in 1996, she approached a local gallery about a commission. Studying the hens in the farmyard, she produced four figures, each in a different medium: wire, twigs, cement and wool. The simple black wirework outline featuring a red comb was by far the most successful – and her obsession with the medium began. While she worked in bars and cafés, Celia crafted wirework chickens in a variety of designs and sizes over the next two years, selling them in shops and galleries.

Shortly after the move to her pretty terraced cottage in Box in 1998, a village on the steep, hilly outskirts of Bath, she made an entire flock of hens for an exhibition – the publicity for which led to an inundation of orders, meaning that she could afford to take a part-time position at an arts marketing business and concentrate on crafting the increasingly popular birds. Her work was in such demand that halfway through a spell travelling the world with her now husband Peter in 2000, she returned to her parents' farm to carry out a large order of cockerels for restaurant chain Nando's. "I made 20 sculptures in four weeks – I was working round the clock," she recalls. Rejoining Peter in New Zealand, Celia began to study the country's rich birdlife, making the transition from sculptures of domestic poultry to wild birds.

On her return to the UK, she turned her attention to British wildfowl and, today, Celia is busily working on commissions and meeting orders for her covetable wirework sculptures – from tiny copper curlews to vast tangles of starlings in flight. She spends up to one day every week at Slimbridge: "I can be really close to the birds there – they're so tame." She has recently bought a telescope, which, set up on a tripod in a hide, allows her to watch a bird such as a heron in great detail while her hands are free to 'sketch' in wire – a mesmerising spectacle in itself. "Observing a bird in its natural environment is the best way to get an idea of its shape and behaviour," Celia explains. "So sculpting outside just seems natural."

In her search for new subject matter, she travels all over the British Isles. In November 2005, she was granted a bursary by the Wildfowl & Wetlands Trust and the Society of Wildlife Artists to study the whooper swans at Welney in Norfolk. "I went out to the fens to sketch them and set up my studio in one of the hides, where I'd watch them at dusk." Shetland's puffins, razorbills and guillemots lured Celia to the islands where she lived from January to May 2006 as artist in residence at a primary school, introducing the children to her ironwork methods and using her duck-egg blue VW Transporter van as a mobile studio-cum-hide so as not to scare her subjects away. It was here, where fences, not hedges, mark boundaries, that she gathered reams and reams of old, rusty wire. In her studio, metal strands of all thicknesses and colours, from powder-coated white to fiery brass, spill out from shelves of boxes. A reel of gauzy metal, in which she punches holes and sews washers, forms the polka-dot plumage of the guinea fowls that strut about her parents' farm, while black-and-white-patterned kettle flexes will become the plumage of barnacle geese. Celia finds much of her material at a scrapyard in nearby Yeovil, and BT provides her with old coloured telephone wires.

Celia is so enthusiastic about birdlife, her artform and materials, it's hard to imagine her ever running out of ideas. "I'm into waders, such as godwits, at the moment; I like their ridiculously long legs and beaks," she says. "And I want to capture the black and white flicker of lapwings as they fly in the Somerset Levels," she says. She is also keen to explore further the chemistry of all these metals – applying heat, corroding them with water. "But what I'd like most of all," she says, "is to have my own flock of hens to sculpt." 🦅 *Small studies start from £120 (celia-smith.co.uk).*

OPPOSITE, FROM FAR LEFT A Nene goose; finishing a 'sketch' in situ; Celia spends at least one day a week studying birds. "Each time I'm out in the field, I learn more about a bird's movement"

# DESIGNS
## *from the islands*

*The natural patterns of Orkney's wonderful wild flowers and grasses inspire
Sarah Johnston's beautiful hand-printed fabrics and accessories*

WORDS BY **LOUISE ELLIOTT** | PHOTOGRAPHS BY **BRENT DARBY**

THIS PAGE AND OPPOSITE
Sarah's graphic patterns
are printed in an array of
fresh, contemporary
colours onto Scottish linen

262   HANDMADE STYLE Country Living

The largely treeless landscape of Orkney, with its expansive blue skies and green farmland, edged by an undulating coastline of sand and rock, emphasises the glorious array of wild flowers that flourishes on the islands. In every field, hedgerow and humble roadside verge, drifts of marsh orchids, buttercups, red campion, poppies, heather and yellow irises create a colourful canvas alongside swaying grasses and lacy umbellifers. Textile designer Sarah Johnston appreciates the individual beauty of each one on her regular walks and captures their forms in her stylised fabric prints. "There are so many different habitats here," she says.

Marram Studio, the business Sarah set up in 2004 after completing a degree in textile design at Glasgow School of Art, is named after the native grass that grows in the islands' sand dunes, and embodies her passion for Orkney's flora. "My fascination with detail, colour and decoration began when I took up photography at school and recorded arrangements of pebbles, driftwood and flowers in the wild or the ferns, dahlias and fuchsia hedges in my father's garden," she recalls.

Setting up her own business has allowed Sarah to concentrate on the nature-inspired images she loves to create. "I didn't like the thought of being in a large company and churning out work," she explains. "I needed to follow my own aesthetic and be involved at every stage from initial concept to finished product." She started working from her parents' home in the fishing port of Stromness, and her first collection was a range of jacquard silk and cotton cushions and throws woven on the mainland but made up by Sarah. By December 2005, she needed more space to meet the demand raised by selling at local fairs and craft shops, and leapt at the chance to rent a studio in the old Stromness Academy, a grey-stone Victorian building on a hill behind the waterfront. Today, she divides her time between Glasgow and Orkney.

Each new pattern begins with a photo of her chosen flower, grass or natural find followed by a rough paper sketch later re-drawn onto her computer. "This allows me to move the shapes around to find the best arrangement and I can play with different colours, scales and details to achieve the strongest image." The digital image is then printed onto a sheet of acetate and transferred to a hand-held printing screen using photographic emulsion. Next, Sarah tapes squares of fabric onto her five-metre-long table, and special water-based ink is mixed by eye to create a depth of colour. Using a squeegee, she deftly runs the ink up and down the printing screen, being careful not to flood the fabric.

With her textile training, the initial parts of the process were almost second nature to Sarah but she has had to develop her sewing skills along the way, making her cushions, bags and purses on an easy-to-use Bernina machine in her studio. She has also developed a keen eye for the look of the textiles and accessories. Each item has a simple, retro-influenced design that brings out the beauty of her motifs, from bags, cushions and purses to T-shirts and tea towels. She has also created a range of cards bearing images of teasels, umbellifers, poppies, orchids and lilies printed onto cotton paper, made from waste fibres, using a vintage letterpress.

A pinboard in her studio displays ideas in the pipeline and she plans to produce lengths of fabric for curtains and soft furnishings. "The internet opened up the possibilities of running a business on an island," she says, "and no matter how busy I am, I always make time to enjoy Orkney's world of nature." ↵
*Marram Studio (0141 445 2731; marramstudio.com)*

# Silver
# SERVICE

Graham Stewart's elegantly shaped designs capture
the essence of the countryside around his Perthshire home,
and are a shining example of the silversmith's craft

WORDS BY **KATE LANGRISH** | PHOTOGRAPHS BY **CRISTIAN BARNETT**

You don't have to look far to see where silversmith Graham Stewart draws his inspiration. On the windowsill of his Dunblane studio, a candleholder of a small silver bird perches on a rowan leaf – just outside the window, a wren hops among the branches of the same tree. "I often find ideas when we're out walking the dogs," Graham says. "My wife Elizabeth will point out an interesting seed head or perhaps the shape of a crocus flower, then I'll go home and start sketching out designs."

The creation of Graham's pieces is as organic as the inspiration, but they are not detailed wildlife replicas. Instead, it's the essence of nature he captures – the curve of a heron's wing, the flick of a salmon's tail or the flow of a stream. But this is not ornamental silverware; Graham's work is made to be used. And so his graceful, long-necked jugs have spouts that pour precisely, a set of trophies he created for a food awards ceremony incorporate a working ladle, while his whisky tumblers are so perfectly balanced, they stand unaided and wobble-free on a table.

This combination of practicality and creativity runs in the family, it seems; Graham's father trained as an instrument maker in the army and became an industrial engineer, but was also a dab hand with a hammer and anvil. "He taught evening classes locally in silversmithing," Graham says. "I had a music lesson at the same

THIS PAGE Graham starts by sketching his designs. OPPOSITE Much of his work is commissioned to mark a special occasion; the 17th-century gallery, studio and workshop

Graham will often sit down with customers at the gallery and start sketching out ideas on the back of a postcard

time, and used to come in at the end for a lift home. I was meant to sit at the back and do my homework, but I was much more interested in the class."

His father's old workshop is still in the garden behind the 17th-century rust-coloured building that houses Graham's gallery, studio and his own workshop, which is down a set of steep stone steps in the basement. The workshop walls are covered with neat lines of planishing hammers hanging on racks – many of the tools were his father's and some even belonged to his great-grandfather, who had a smithy on his farm. Huge anvils stand alongside upturned elm logs with scooped-out hollows, which Graham uses to 'raise' silver bowls, while curved chunks are missing from the edges of the work benches where he can bend the spouts. Underneath is an assortment of pebble-smooth steel, which he uses to mould his bowls and jugs.

He is not alone in the workshop: there is jeweller Norrie; fellow silversmith Neil; and lastly, Graham's brother, Iain, a retired engineer and deviser of solutions to all technical problems. "Everyone brings different skills to help produce the end package," Graham explains. "Iain is really good at cooking up different ways of doing things; he makes a lot of the instruments we need before we can even start working with the silver."

Upstairs is the quiet sanctuary of his studio. A huge window and workbench stretch across the length of the room, with a view out to the garden and his father's old workshop. It's here that he sits and sketches out new ideas, and the workbench is dotted with seed heads, scraps of paper with drawings of fish and leaves, and practice runs of his fluid freehand lettering. Sitting over in the corner are Yoshi and Louie, Graham and Elizabeth's two whippets. "The dogs haven't made it into silver yet," Graham says. But, as Elizabeth points out with a smile, his tall jugs bear more than a passing resemblance to the graceful necks and slender tails of the two dogs looking on quietly as Graham works.

That Graham is inspired by his surroundings is clear, but what is less obvious is the input he draws from his customers. The ground floor of the building houses the gallery, displaying both his work and that of other craftspeople he and Elizabeth admire. It's a very warm and inviting room, with wonky wooden floors and work displayed in a way that encourages customers to touch and hold it. "People feel comfortable enough to come in and describe what they want Graham to make. He then sits down with them and starts sketching things out on the back of a postcard," Elizabeth explains.

This skill is not lost on his customers, some of whom regularly return to commission something for a special occasion – a wedding gift of an elegant jug, perhaps, and bowls engraved for a baby's birth. "We have one couple who travel every year from Cambridge on their anniversary," Elizabeth says. But Christmas is always the busiest time of year. "Silver is the perfect material for celebrating," Graham says. ✒

*Graham Stewart Silversmith, 91-95 High Street, Dunblane, Perthshire (01786 825244; grahamstewartsilver smith.co.uk). Prices for spoons start at around £250 and for tumblers from £400.*

# BOLT *from the* BLUE

The last woad mill in Britain
closed its doors in the 1930s. Now
a Norfolk farmer is spearheading
a revival of this crop, using its
distinctive indigo dye to colour textiles and accessories

WORDS BY **KITTY CORRIGAN** | PHOTOGRAPHS BY **ANDREW MONTGOMERY**

Mention "woad" and most people think of ancient Britons painting their bodies blue before charging into battle. So it's a surprise to discover it growing on a farm in Norfolk, in the very region once ruled by Boadicea, the warrior queen.

The plant itself looks unremarkable, like a cross between spinach and sugar beet, with a yellow flower (it belongs to the mustard family) but the dye, indigo, extracted from it was for centuries highly prized. The blue threads in the Bayeux tapestry were dyed with woad, and this is the only colour not to have faded over 900 years. The Saxon green garb of Robin Hood and his merry men was achieved by dyeing first with a yellow dye called wild mignonette and then with woad.

When the boys in blue – the airforce and police – switched to using synthetic dyes for their uniform in the early 1930s, the last woad mill, in Lincolnshire, closed. But this ancient crop is enjoying a revival as textile artists, fashion designers and home crafters become increasingly interested in natural dyes.

Eleven years ago Ian Howard was growing potatoes, wheat and sugar beet, and had a suckler herd of South Devons, near Dereham in Norfolk, but he became disillusioned with farming and decided to sell a large part of his land and invest in woad cultivation on the remaining 37 hectares. Now he is Britain's only commercial grower of woad. Harvesting is from July until October – each tonne of leaves produces two kilos of pigment.

"I am fascinated by the alchemy of the dyeing process," Ian says. "When cloth is dipped into a vat of woad dye, it first turns yellow, then within minutes changes to green, turquoise and finally deep blue." The transformation occurs on contact with the air (oxidisation), but to visiting schoolchildren it's magic, and adults attending his workshops are equally amazed.

Woad is a native European herb, *Isatis tinctoria*, and produces the same pigment as its former rival, *Indigofera tinctoria*, an Asian import that

was deemed such a threat to the woad industry in the 16th century that an international group called the Woadites tried to block its use, calling it "devil food", but, since it was cheaper, it gradually became the dye of choice.

Ian's wife Bernadette, formerly a PA in a large department store, uses her organisational and financial skills to help with the production and marketing of the woad items sold by mail order. After researching the opportunities, Ian and Bernadette decided to focus on homeware and now sell a collection of towels, rugs, throws, toiletries and fashion accessories including knitwear, with yarn from, appropriately, Blueface Leicester sheep. The dyed yarn is wound on to spools or "cheeses" and sold direct to the customer or made up into garments by outworkers locally. Other items are made with cotton, silk, linen, alpaca – and bamboo. When mixed 70/30 with cotton, this gives the perfect texture, strength and absorbency for towelling. At first, Ian dyed everything himself but this became impractical as the business grew. However, smaller items are still made and dyed on the farm. As word spreads, more and more people are approaching him for advice. He would like to supply natural dye for designer jeans and also pursue his interest in pharmaceuticals, as scientists investigate use of the plant in a cancer-fighting drug.

As a keen Norwich City football fan, Ian has designed a silk scarf in the club colours, trialling another heritage crop, weld, to produce yellow and overdyeing with woad for the green. He is also a vintage car collector, and his pride and joy is a 1933 Austin 7 that he bought 25 years ago. "I'd never part with it," he says. "I stripped every nut and bolt, and worked on it until it was in perfect working order." Its colour just happens to be indigo blue. *For information on workshops and products, see thewoadcentre.co.uk.*

OPPOSITE The woad leaves are steeped, baked and ground to extract the indigo dye. THIS PAGE Harvesting the crop

WORDS BY **PAULA McWATERS**
PHOTOGRAPHS BY
**ANDREW MONTGOMERY**

# Impressions
## of NATURE

Claire Powell uses plants picked from her cottage garden
to create uniquely patterned pottery – every piece
beautiful to look at and practical to use

A small patch of a flowerbed in her parents' garden is where Claire Powell's love of both plants and pottery began. She started growing country flowers such as sweet peas and forget-me-nots when she was six years old. Digging over the earth, Claire also discovered fragments of pottery, which she kept as if they were treasure. "I still have many of these pieces now," she says. "They started a collection that I've added to all my life."

The two passions that were sparked in childhood shape Claire's life in the village of Frocester, Gloucestershire, today. The garden around her pale-green workshop is as important as her clay and kiln: she hand-decorates her distinctive earthenware bowls, jugs, mugs and cheese domes with the leaves of cottage garden favourites. Hardy geraniums, delphiniums, lupins, nasturtiums and roses flourish here alongside willow and silver birch trees.

These fresh leaves serve as stencils over which Claire sprays the glaze onto her ceramics. "I overlay the leaves to give a three-dimensional effect and each one can be used only once, so no two pots are ever the same." The foliage is chosen for its differing qualities: lupins give a star effect whereas herb Robert and cow parsley create a lacier, more ethereal pattern. Each piece can have up to four or five layers of glaze in varying shades of blue, green or both. "The shapes are dream-like, giving an Impressionist effect as the glaze melts."

Claire's career in pottery started in 1970 when she did a ceramic design course, followed by making glazes for Tingewick Pottery – a family-owned business in Buckinghamshire. "We sourced glazes to make slipware lamps in wonderful vibrant colours," she says. "It gave me a taste for experimenting and I started making my own pots. Also I'm quite impatient and throwing gives quick results."

She began to develop her stencilling method in the mid-1980s while living

on a farm in France with her then husband and two children. "I found painting with glaze difficult," she says. "Some friends suggested I try a spray gun instead, so I began stencilling around leaves." She sold her pottery at a local market and it proved a great success. Later, returning to Britain, Claire retrained as a teacher to support the family and her pottery became little more than a hobby, until nine years ago when she met her husband Paul and moved to the Cotswolds.

Today, a pond with moorhens, a vegetable patch and roses provide an inspiring view from her workshop. Claire starts with terracotta or white earthenware clay, judging each piece by eye and working it up on the wheel using gentle fingertip pressure. "The hand on the inside does all the work while the hand on the outside provides support," she explains, as her wheel whirs round. "I like to make practical pieces. People must be able to use them, not just look at them."

The popular blue and turquoise glazes she first developed still influence the palette of her work and she mixes up her own distinctive colours. "Every so often, I try out new colours and finishes," she says. "But these are my signature shades. I have customers who might buy a bowl one year and come back for a cheese dome the next, so it's important to have continuity."

She spends two to three days a week making the pots and biscuit-firing them, followed by a day deciding on patterns and then glazing. "A steep-sided bowl demands something large and bold," she explains, "whereas a small piece needs a more delicate pattern." With a trug over her arm, she goes in search of the right specimens, returning to the workshop with around 30-40 to experiment with. After glazing but before second firing, the pottery looks a dull matt grey and it is not until the bowls and jugs emerge from the kiln that the colours are revealed. "The excitement I feel when I open the kiln is still as strong today," she says.

The unique quality of Claire's work has attracted a loyal following and she sells her ceramics at fairs, at Stroud Farmers' Market and from her studio. Despite her prolific output, Claire is in no danger of running out of ideas. "There's always some kind of plant life to use," she explains. "Even in winter there are allium seed heads." In summer, though, the garden is in its full glory and Claire is surrounded by subject matter. "At this time of year, it's impossible to go on holiday – I can't tear myself away." *Claire Powell Pottery, Frocester, Stonehouse, Gloucestershire (01453 827975; claire-powell-pottery.co.uk). Studio visits by appointment.*

# *Printed*
# TREASURES

*Meet Georgia Wilkinson, who creates 1960s-inspired fabrics with a flora and fauna theme from a former cricket pavilion in North Yorkshire*

WORDS BY **LISA SYKES** | PHOTOGRAPHS BY **ALUN CALLENDER**

A flagstone path through an apple orchard and wild-flower meadow leads to a 1930s cricket pavilion. In the field beyond the veranda, sheep graze and a peahen's plumed fascinator bobs through yellowing grasses – a tranquillity only heightened by the sounds of birds on the breeze. Welcome to the workspace of Georgia Wilkinson.

Given her natural surroundings, it isn't surprising that Georgia's striking, 1960s-influenced textiles feature stylised images of flora and fauna. Magpies, ladybirds, bees and, for her latest collection, peonies, pansies and poppies, jump out from the fabric rolls and products stored on shelves around the pavilion. To the left was the visiting team's dressing room, now the HQ of Georgia's business, Jorja Wilkinson

## "My work is influenced by the 1960s but brought up to date with a crisp palette and striking repeats"

Design. It's also where she creates her bold, quirky motifs before, in the home side's area opposite, turning them into cushions, lampshades, tea towels and noticeboards, which are sold through her website and in shops nationwide. "My work is influenced by the bold, clean lines of 1960s wallpapers and ceramics but brought up to date with a crisp palette and striking repeats," she says.

Georgia has been based inside the pavilion since 2009, when she returned to her parents' 511-acre arable farm in the Vale of York, following two years as a designer in London where she worked on designs for companies such as Bennison, Vanessa Arbuthnott and Lewis & Wood. Much of the inspiration for her designs comes from the British countryside with hares, capercaillies, red kites, corncrakes and great bitterns featuring among her collection.

The rolls of cotton flat-weave fabrics are all produced by a company in Macclesfield, but Georgia screenprints the linen for the tea towels and some of her cushions by hand on her parents' kitchen table. "I air dry the fabric and set the design in my gran's old ironing press – it's very low tech," she says. In an array of wonderful colours, any piece by Georgia will add an eye-catching, individual element to a room. The only trouble is deciding which one to have. ✦

*Jorja Wilkinson Design, Pilmoor Grange, Helperby, North Yorkshire (07894 205491; jorjawilkinson design.co.uk).*

# Fired up for the future

Richard Miller has created an inspiring pottery business based on artisan skills and his passion for clay

WORDS BY **LOUISE ELLIOTT** | PHOTOGRAPHS BY **EMMA LEE**

Richard Miller is a breath of fresh air in the world of traditional artisan crafts. Since his early twenties, he has been running his own successful business producing handmade tiles and ceramics that will bring individual beauty to even the plainest space. Since taking over Froyle Tiles in 2005, then based in the Hampshire village of Froyle, he has had to learn fast. "After finishing my degree in ceramics at Farnham University, I had been working as a jobbing potter," he recalls. "Then a friend told me that Froyle Tiles was closing down and I thought I could just buy some of the equipment. But after having a go at making the tiles myself, I loved the process so much that I decided to take over the small amount of debt the business had and keep it going." And when the lease on the existing workshop came to an end, Richard knew exactly where he wanted to relocate: "The Farnham Buildings Preservation Trust had been renovating Farnham Pottery in the village of Wrecclesham in Surrey for the past ten years, and I had run courses and workshops there. I thought it would be really exciting to bring commercial pottery-making back to the site, and be part of recreating a sense of history."

It's easy to understand why he felt so enthused by the tradition of this unique pottery with its cluster of red-brick buildings made from local clay and ironwork forged on site. Founded by Absalom Harris in 1872, in its heyday it had four working bottle kilns, its own pits and railway to deliver clay to the pottery, and up to 30 workers. As well as architectural fittings, it made domesticware and garden pots, supplying shops such as Heal's and Liberty, with the Queen Mother, Gertrude Jekyll and Sir Edward Lutyens among its customers. By the early 20th century, the pottery was at the heart of the West Surrey Arts & Crafts movement and many of the building's original features capture the mood of this period – the decorative archways, chimneys and clock, the sgraffito lettering of the

THIS PAGE Richard uses an old pug mill to extrude the clay into a block; many of the decorative designs are inspired by nature

family name, the tiled roofs and the terracotta windowframes.

The pottery provided the perfect premises while Richard was building the business but the success of his handmade creations meant that he needed more room for a shop, showroom and extra staff, and he has now moved to a larger space in the nearby village of Hambledon. But many of the processes he uses are still the same as those put into practice at the Victorian pottery. First, an old-fashioned pug mill extrudes lumps of white stoneware clay into blocks to remove any bubbles of air. These are then sliced by hand while still soft before being shaped inside a slap-mould, trimmed and dried. "Most tiles today

are machine-made from low-fired earthenware or terracotta, but ours are handmade stoneware, which means they are frost-proof," Richard says.

Glazes mixed from natural oxides are applied before firing to give a better fusion between the clay and the finish, with Richard achieving a wonderful array of shades from rich deep plums and moss greens to soft sea blues. Many of his tiles are sold to Fired Earth and a number of independent tile shops. As well as the standard range, Richard, now helped by three full-time potters, works to commission, restores old designs and produces architectural pieces. "The restoration work throws up a lot of challenges," he says. "People often come in with one cracked tile

from a fireplace surround and ask me to match it – working by hand means we can produce a wide variety of colours, shapes and sizes."

The range of pieces sold in his shop reflect Richard's desire to run a creative, collaborative business. So there are tiles decorated by other artists, including beautiful bird, bee and foliage motifs by one of his university tutors, garden planters with the distinctive rope designs and Tudor rose used by the original pottery, as well as hand-carved ceramic house signs and Richard's own wood-fired bottles. "My love of working with clay inspires everything I do," he says. 🦆
*Froyle Tiles, Hambledon Pottery, The Old Coal Yard, Hambledon, Surrey (01428 684111).*

THIS PAGE He works with great precision at all stages of the process to create the beautifully coloured tiles

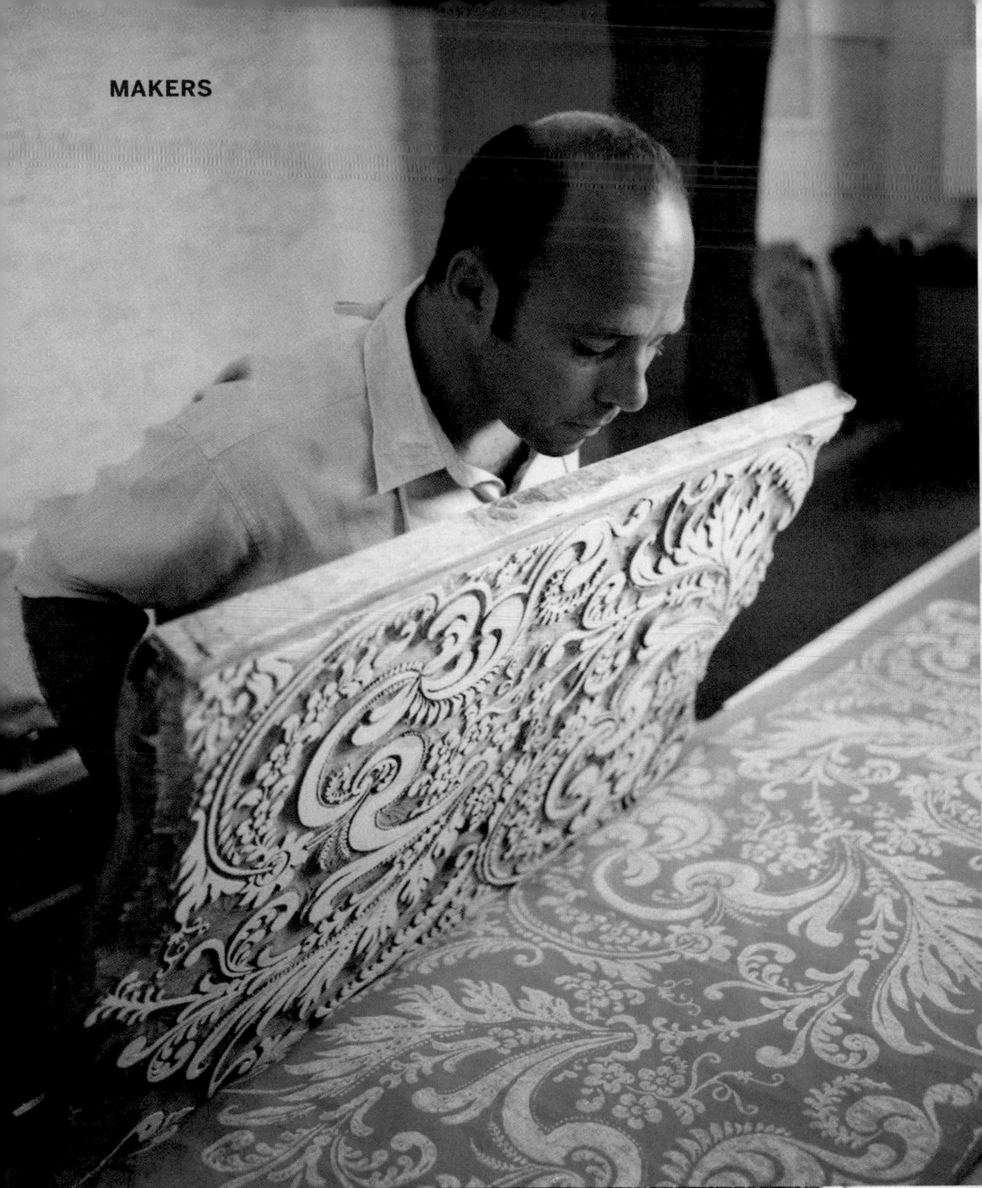

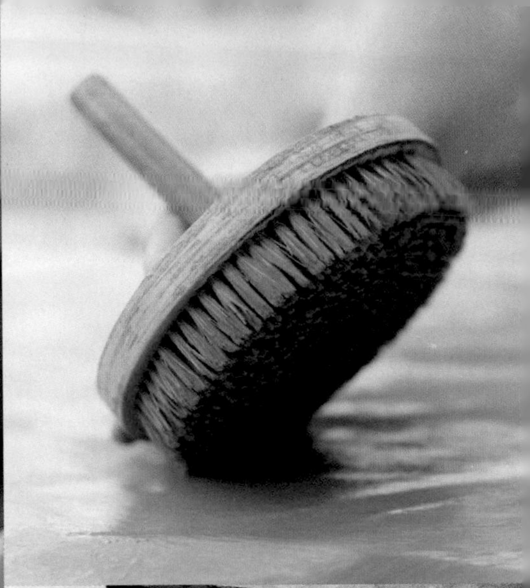

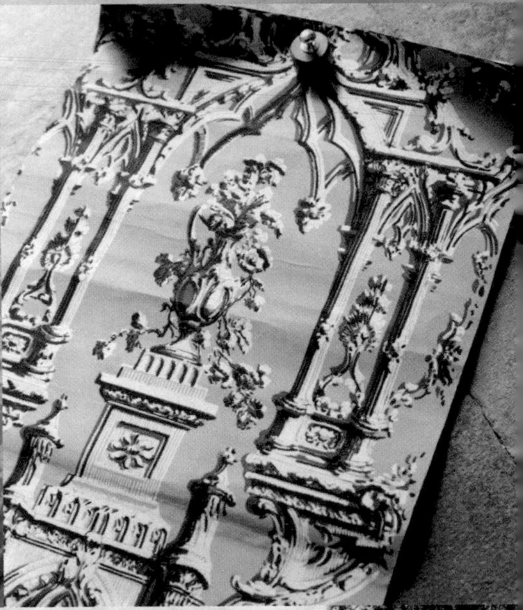

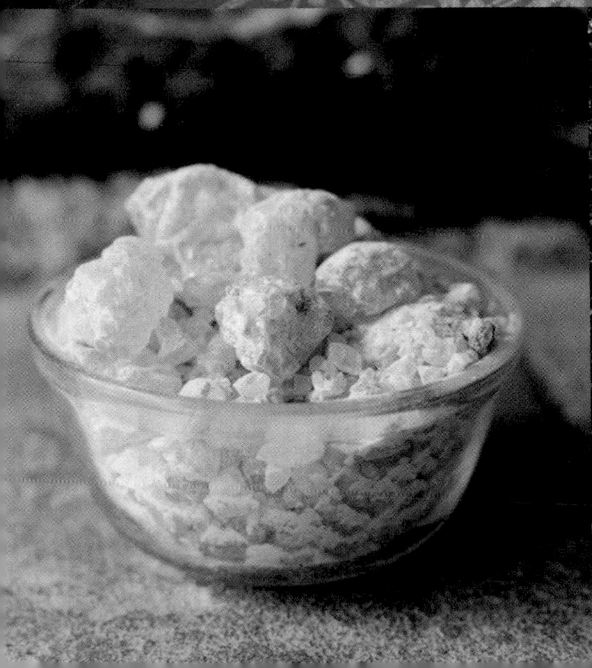

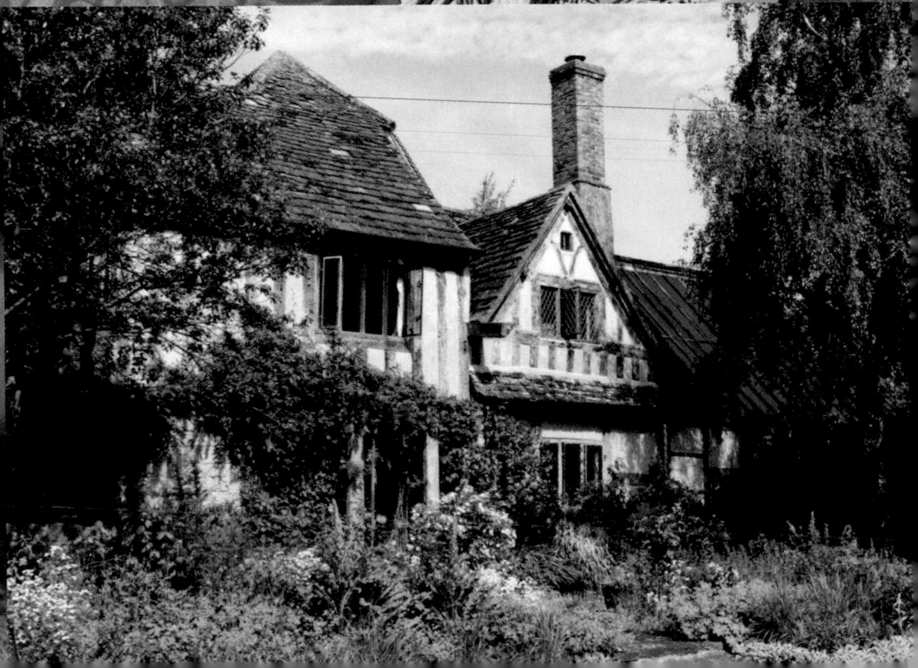

WORDS BY **CAROLINE ATKINS**
PHOTOGRAPHS BY
**ANDREW MONTGOMERY**

# *Patterns* of the past

*Using age-old techniques that date back to the 18th century,
Allyson McDermott painstakingly repairs and recreates
exquisite hand-blocked wallpapers with an authentic flourish*

THIS PAGE Pigments are
finely ground using a
glass pestle. OPPOSITE
Allyson matches
patterns and colours
on identical paper

In another life, Allyson McDermott would have been a scientist. Her delight in forensic analysis is more usually found in academic research than creative design. It was horrible, she remembers, having to choose between science and history at her prep school: in the end she opted for history, inspired by the wonderful Arts and Crafts wallpapers and carvings of the school's Lake District building, and went on to study history of art. But she never abandoned her interest in scientific technique and, after training in watercolour restoration, she switched from paintings to wallpapers. Now, she has the best of both worlds – a part-medieval, part-Tudor house, with its own history to peel away, and a laboratory in her garden: the studio where she analyses and recreates wallpaper designs dating back to the 17th century.

She's been here for three years now, establishing her life on a triangle of Gloucestershire farmland that juts out into the Severn. Moving from Petworth in West Sussex, where the National Trust had been both her landlord and her client, she transplanted her entire family (including her parents). She's now dug herself firmly into the Forest of Dean community, taking on local people as apprentices in her studio, cutting local wood to make her printing blocks, employing local carpenters to carve them – even using local sheep to supply fleece for her flock papers.

Allyson's studio, a converted milking parlour across the drive, is equipped with the high-specification microscopic equipment she needs to identify the pigments, papers, glues and varnishes used for the historic designs she works from. It's a challenge she says she never tires of. "When I qualified in conservation, in the early 1980s, 'works of art on paper' meant watercolours. After you've done your first couple of thousand watercolours, you do start thinking there must be more to life." So when Allyson was asked to repair fire-damaged French and Chinese wallpapers, she leapt at the chance to combine her conservation expertise with her knowledge of design and manufacturing history. "I love the fact that it's three-dimensional, not just flat art," she says. "You have to think about the history and structure of the building, as well as the paper itself."

Also, terrifyingly, the paper has to be removed from the wall: the plan chest in Allyson's studio holds delicate fragments – some faded, some torn or water-stained – that have been lifted off, layer by layer, from historic houses in the UK and across Europe. In some cases, they will simply be washed and repaired. In others, where the damage to the original paper is more extensive, the fragments will be matched and copied, their pattern faithfully reproduced with identical colours on identical paper, and the whole

"I love the fact that it's not just flat art. You have to think about the history of the building, as well as the paper itself"

wall pieced together in a sort of historical jigsaw, with the new pieces indistinguishable from the old.

Her first printing project was an 18th-century wallpaper created to match remnants that had been found stuffed up a chimney at Temple Newsam, a Tudor-Jacobean mansion in Leeds. Researching from craftsmen's manuals and historic houses, she worked out how to 'pounce' (or pinprick) the design onto a paper template, then untangle the different elements of the pattern, transferring each one onto a fruit-wood printing block and from there onto paper. That first print took six blocks (each of which she carved herself) and three colours. But the technique worked and gave her the courage to try her first flock paper. The resulting design – handmade linen paper varnished green and embellished with a rich leaf pattern – hangs with other finished papers along one side of the studio, all proud trophies of successful challenges of the past 20 years.

The other members of Allyson's campaign, recruited from the nearby village of Newnham, are picking up their ▷

THIS PAGE Allyson takes
on local people as
apprentices; analysing
patterns under a
magnifying glass;
carved wooden blocks.
OPPOSITE A wallpaper
is hand-finished

conservation skills at the sharp end: learning how to tear panels of paper to the right size and join them by hand to form wall-height drops; mixing buckets of powdered pigments with animal glue; grounding the paper in textured colour applied with circular brushes; and coating heavy wooden blocks with paint and transferring their patterns onto the paper in a finely judged sequence of pressing and lifting. Dave, who used to be a builder, has already started to carve pattern blocks; Kathryn, his fiancée, is learning how to analyse the original papers under the microscope – which is where it all starts, Allyson explains. The irony is that, in order to work out how to reproduce papers by traditional techniques, Allyson has to use technology the 18th- and 19th-century designers could never have imagined. In retracing their steps, she's acquired endless respect for those craftsmen. She and her team know how many things can go awry: achieving a perfectly printed sheet involves every pattern block being carved to the right design and depth, the press being positioned to an accuracy of millimetres and the blocks being lifted cleanly off, without any sideways slip.

At Uppark in West Sussex, where the National Trust called her in to repair the fire-damaged print room, the wallpaper behind the prints was deep crimson, in contrast to the exposed areas, which had faded to a series of paler shades. Allyson had to print different-coloured papers so the room could be recreated as it was before the fire, using materials that will fade at the same rate as the undamaged paper. It's almost like grafting new skin onto a living organism. "For the deep red behind the pictures we used cochineal, so if it's exposed again, it will fade like the rest of the room," she says. "Where original parts survive, you have to match them."

The same rules apply to ordinary houses and stately homes. Allyson will print designs to recreate a 1930s semi or a mid-Victorian terrace (any colour, any quantity, as long as she has a sample to match). "Only when a room is decorated in its historic manner do you understand the impact it would once have had and fully appreciate the skills of the original craftsmen," she says.

In her own home, she's still uncovering history, leaving walls unpainted until she is sure of how the light strikes them, then limewashing them in natural pigments. Downstairs, willow screens divide some of the rooms. A medieval wall painting is temporarily protected by glass, and woodworm holes in the beams trace their own history. The structure feels exposed and honest, so Allyson can see what she's dealing with, just as she can when working at her microscope. Its sparsely decorated quality is a perfect backdrop to the rich patterns she creates in her studio. "We do have deadlines," she says, "but we also have time to think. This is the most wonderful place to do just that." ✍
*Papers cost from £45 per linear metre (01594 510003; allysonmcdermott.com).*

# Subscribe to *Country Living* magazine

# HALF PRICE*

In every issue of *Country Living* you'll find a wealth of ideas for your home and garden, learn about traditional crafts, discover the best rural businesses and enjoy delicious recipes using seasonal produce.

## Great reasons to subscribe

- **JUST £23.40** for your first 12 issues*
- **ONLY £1.95** per copy (normal price £3.99)
- **SAVE 22%** on every issue thereafter*
- **EXCLUSIVE** subscriber-only offers and discounts
- **FREE** delivery direct to your door

**ONLY £1.95 PER COPY**

Subscribe online – it's quick and easy

# qualitymagazines.co.uk/cl/hs913

Call today and quote code: KCL10084

# 0844 848 1601†

Lines open weekdays 8am-9.30pm; Saturdays 8am-4pm

†BT landline calls to 0844 numbers will cost no more than 5p per minute; calls from mobiles and other networks usually cost more.